THE
LEISURE
Crisis

J O H N   O S W A L T

Though intended for personal reading and profit, this book
is part of the Victor Adult Elective Series and therefore
is also intended for group study. A Leader's Guide with
Victor Multiuse Transparency Masters is available from
your local bookstore.

VICTOR BOOKS™
A DIVISION OF SCRIPTURE PRESS PUBLICATIONS INC.
USA CANADA ENGLAND

Scripture quotations marked NIV are from
the *Holy Bible, New International Version,* ©
1973, 1978, 1984, International Bible Society.
Used by permission of Zondervan Bible
Publishers. Quotations marked NKJV are
from *The New King James Version.* © 1979,
1980, 1982, Thomas Nelson, Inc., Publishers.
Quotations marked RSV are from the *Revised
Standard Version of the Bible,* © 1946, 1952,
1971, 1973. Quotations marked PH are from J.B.
Phillips: *The New Testament in Modern
English,* Revised Edition, © J.B. Phillips, 1958,
1960, 1972, permission of Macmillan
Publishing Co. and Collins Publishers.
Quotations marked KJV are from the *King
James Version.*

Recommended Dewey Decimal Classification: 301.57

Suggested Subject Heading: LEISURE

Library of Congress Catalog Card Number: 86-63148

ISBN: 0-89693-241-9

C O N T E N T S

For

Elizabeth, Andrew, and Peter

who have taught me much about leisure

ACKNOWLEDGMENTS

It is a pleasure to recognize several people who have had a significant part in bringing these ideas into print. First is Dr. Wayne Goodwin, faculty colleague at Asbury Theological Seminary and good friend, who requested that I put together a seminar on leisure for the annual Minister's Conference and encouraged me to believe that I had something to say on the subject. Then Mrs. Sandra Higgs and Miss Helen Pielemeier made sense of my taped words and produced a workable transcript. Later Miss Pielemeier typed an edited version of the transcript. Mrs. Carole Sanderson Streeter and Mr. Mark Sweeney of Victor Books have been unfailingly encouraging in their belief that the transcript could indeed be turned into a book. Professor William Toll found a way to transfer files stored in Asbury College's mainframe computer to discs usable in my personal computer. Finally, thanks to my wife Karen who has good-naturedly put up with, and even supported, my leisure-time interests and hobbies. Thanks to each one. Your labors are not in vain in the Lord!

INTRODUCTION

When I tell my friends that I, a college president at the time of this writing, am writing a book on leisure, they laugh. A college president write on leisure? Of all the professions that know next to nothing about leisure, surely this one is near the top of the list!

This little incident reflects the central theme of this book. We live in a time that offers opportunities for leisure that would have been unthinkable even a hundred years ago. Yet we seem to have much less free time than our ancestors.

My father will be 90 years old this year. During his lifetime he has watched a revolution occur. For the first time in human history we have a society where most people do not need to spend all their time supplying basic necessities. That was not the case in 1895. To be sure, there were leisured classes then, as there have always been. But it was still true 90 years ago, as it has been since the dawn of time, that the masses needed to work 10 to 14 hours per day, six days a week, in order to supply basic life necessities. That is no longer true. In the 90-year period of my father's life we have come to the place in the West, at least, where the vast majority can supply basic necessities in a fraction of their time. We face a radically new situation. We no longer need to fill our time with work.

With what then *will* we fill our time? And how? To be sure, there is no dearth of possibilities. Far from it! If we need to work less than ever before to supply basic needs, it may also be argued that we are busier than ever before. There seem to be more things clamoring for our time than we can possibly handle. My laughing friends come to mind. "You? Write a book on leisure? You've got to be kidding!"

This is the crisis of our times. To be sure, the towering crisis is the political and military one. Will we as a race be able to avoid nuclear annihilation on the one hand or ideologically based tyranny on the other? But supposing we do—what then? What will the nature of life be? How shall we use our time?

The question is not *whether* we shall fill the time. We will do that, like it or not. No, the question is *how* we shall fill it. Shall we fill it frantically, fearful of even five minutes with nothing to do? Shall we fill it haphazardly, merely seeking for something that will allow us to escape from the grinding boredom of our existence? Shall we fill it willy-nilly, just doing whatever comes to hand next? Or shall we take advantage of this new freedom from the need for dawn-to-dusk labor to find ways to become more truly human, more deeply Christian?

I believe we can do this, but we must seize the opportunity. If we do not, the mediocre will crowd out the best as surely as weeds will take over a flower garden. More than that, we must seize this opportunity for Christ.

What shall we do? Shall we bemoan the passing of the "good old days"? Or shall we, by God's grace, seek and find ways to adapt eternal truth to new situations? Surely this latter way has always been God's way and the secret of the church's survival. Infinitely creative, God has continually found ways to draw the poison from an alien culture and clothe Himself in its forms. And why not? This is the very essence of the Incarnation.

But this way of adapting the culture can be a dangerous one. Again and again throughout history the angels must have held their breath, and sometimes they have surely wept, as they have watched the church seeking to envelop culture. For it is entirely possible—indeed it has happened with regularity—that instead of the church taking over the culture, the culture will swallow up the church.

That possibility is before us here. How easily we may delude ourselves into thinking that we are adapting the Christian message to the leisure culture in order to transform that culture, when in fact we are giving up fundamental truths in order to conform to it. We must guard against that, but I believe we *can* guard against it and that the times demand that we make the attempt. Unless we do succeed in putting the Gospel in terms that speak to a leisure culture and address its concerns, we will be increasingly out of touch and unable to be agents of this culture's redemption.

If we are to have any hope of making leisure a more humanizing experience rather than a dehumanizing one, we must come to some healthy understanding of the concept. Primarily, the idea is a negative one today. It is not doing something. To an alarming extent it is caught up in passivity. The growth of spectator sports is one manifestation of this. A much more alarming manifestation is the voyeurism that accounts for the stellar increase in pornography in this country. But leisure at its heart is not negative. Leisure is the freedom to pursue an art or a skill that is not a means to an end. Instead that activity is an end in itself, and by pursuing it we will become more of that which is truly human. Human beings alone have decorated their tools and have sought pleasing forms for their vessels. They alone have made songs and poems for the sheer joy of it. We have the opportunity to amplify our uniqueness by leaps and bounds.

Think of it! Our age gets to venture down ways that no human beings have ever walked before. We have the opportunity to set up the road signs for untold generations after us. We can point out the high roads and the swamps. But will we? If we will not or cannot, the indications are all too clear. A frantic boredom is all about us, and in terror of it we turn increasingly to the forgetfulness and release of more and more intricate technologies and more and more powerful chemicals. But we need not! There is the tragedy. If our spirits are equal to the challenge—and certainly God's Spirit is equal—the door is open for us to rediscover our true humanity as never before. Let's walk through it!

As a first step and to get you thinking for yourself about this issue, take a couple of minutes now to answer some questions. Don't worry, you can't flunk! So be perfectly honest with yourself.

1. How do you define the word *leisure?*
2. How do you feel about leisure? Why?
3. When do you feel most leisured? Why?
4. Who are the most leisured people you know? Why?
5. If you had five free days and could go anywhere you wanted and do anything you wanted, where would you go and what would you do? Why?
6. On a scale of 1 to 10, with 10 being highest, rate the importance of leisure for a Christian. Why did you choose that particular rating?

PART ONE

LEISURE: WHAT IS THE CRISIS ABOUT?

O N E

WHAT IS LEISURE?

What is leisure? Before we can decide what to do with it, we had better be sure we know what it is. If a small boy were asked what leisure time was, he would probably reply, "That's the time when I can do whatever I want." And I suspect that would define the term pretty well for most of us. Leisure is free time, time that is unencumbered by the "have-to's" or the "ought-to's."

LEISURELY SCHOOL DAYS

But is that all? Isn't there something more to leisure than just "nothing to do"? There certainly is, and like most ideas, we understand it better when we trace it back to its earliest usages. In this case that earliest usage was by the Greeks. Now I think you are in for a surprise. I certainly was. Guess what the Greek word is for leisure? It is *schola*—the root from which our word *school* is derived! Now for most of us the last thing we associate with school is leisure. We think of having to get up in the morning, having to do all those piles of homework, having to learn things whether we liked it or not. But school didn't mean that for the Greeks. What it meant for them was freedom to learn. Only persons who had leisure were free to learn. To have leisure was to have that freedom. The poor fellow, poor woman, who had to work 90 hours a week never had that opportunity. They were never free to look at their world and ask, What does it mean, what's it about? But the person with leisure has that luxury of time to look at the world, to see the relationships among its various parts, to see what it's about, to see where it's going.

What has happened to us? Why don't we think of education in the same way? Well, first of all, I'm sure that Greek schoolboys whose parents required them to go to school looked out the windows of their schoolrooms at a beautiful spring day just as longingly as any modern child does, so we ought not to romanticize the situation too much. On the other hand, the problem of universal compulsory public education is a real one. When we all must do something, whether we have the desire for it or not, it is very difficult for us to see it as a privilege.

Some years ago when a seminary faculty of which I was a member was debating whether to retain Greek as a requirement, I saw this effect of compulsion. I was arguing vigorously that the requirement should be retained. However, one of my colleagues, a professor of Greek, pointed out that I, a professor of Hebrew, which was not required, might not understand the nature of the problem. "You only have students who want to learn the subject in your class," he said. "How would you feel if more than half of your class did not want to be there and if your major task was not teaching the subject, but convincing the majority of the *worth* of the subject?" I had to admit that added a new dimension to the problem. It is a great privilege to know the language in which the New Testament was written. But if I am *required* to know that language, the sense of privilege fast disappears. We voted to retain the Greek requirement, but I gained a new appreciation for the nature of the problem my colleagues faced.

Now I am not in favor of eliminating compulsory public education. Although it creates some problems, its benefits are too great for it to be discarded. What it does mean is that we will have to work harder to recapture the true meaning of leisure. For whatever else our discovery about the meaning of the word teaches us, it teaches us that leisure is the privilege of learning.

As such, leisure is the furthest thing from idleness. It is not doing nothing, which is what idleness is. Rather, it is the use of our free time to become more alive, more vital. To be idle is to fail to look at the world, to fail to appreciate it. It is to fail to become excited by the complex wonders around us. Leisure is looking at the world, appreciating it, becoming excited about it. If we could produce that kind of understanding of and expectation for leisure, I think our society would be vastly different.

Obviously, in the Greek society this kind of leisure was the preserve of the wealthy. Only the wealthy had the freedom to learn, the freedom to look at the world. They had the opportunity to do something most of us, I suspect, are not comfortable with—the opportunity to contemplate. I am not thinking here of the Eastern concept of contemplation whose ultimate goal is detachment from a world that is considered essentially bad. No, I am talking about a view that considers this world to be good and valuable and that is willing to spend time in reflection on and consideration of this world. For most of us who have been raised in an age of pervasive noise and instant analysis, the thought of applying really careful attention to something for a period of time in order to really see or really understand does not sound like leisure. For all too many of us leisure means the opportunity to shut off our minds.

But for our ancestors it was different. Think of Tevya in *Fiddler on the Roof:* "If I were a rich man, what could I do? I could sit in the synagogue all day and read the sacred books and argue with the rabbi." That's leisure. If I were a rich man, I would have the opportunity, the freedom, to think about the world, to think about what matters, to contemplate it. I don't have that freedom now, because I've got to milk my one cow and haul the milk away and keep my wife and family in tow.

CIVILIZATION AND LEISURE

It is in this sense that Aristotle, the great Greek philosopher, argued that leisure is essential to civilization. He believed that civilization could not exist unless a significant group of people had time free from other obligations to look at the world and think about it, time to put it together. And when you consider that for a moment, it's not hard to understand Aristotle's point.

Civilization is more than just a group of people living together. At the least, it is a group of people who are living together in such a way as to achieve their highest potential, both as individuals and as a group. How does that happen? Well, one way to describe it is with the idea of harmony. Harmony means interrelationship of the parts. When you have a choir singing in harmony, then the parts all fit together. But that can't happen unless you know what the parts are and have some idea of how they fit together and what the priorities are. Of course, it also helps if everyone is singing at the same tempo!

But how do you do that in life? How do you find out what

the various parts are and how they fit together in the right sequence and tempo? Only, says Aristotle, if we have the time and the will to step away from the daily grind long enough and frequently enough to get the picture. Most of us, and I would put myself right in the middle of the group, do not feel much harmony in our lives. Why? Because we don't have time, we don't have leisure, to look at the pieces. Instead, we spend a lot of time just pushing our way through the pieces so we can get to the next one. That is not a prescription for harmony but for discord.

And what is the result of all that discord in our social life? A rapid descent to barbarism—or, to put it in biblical terms, the triumph of the flesh over the spirit. The reason for that descent is that without harmony we each do our "own thing," and that is always the most pleasant and least taxing thing. Like weeds, the simplest and most physical of the desires need no cultivation. But the more complex and spiritual possibilities in us, like roses, need constant attention. Without the leisure and the will to tend to them, we cannot maintain them.

IMAGINATION AND CREATIVITY

As I have just been suggesting, not only is harmony essential to civilization, so also is the expression of imagination and creativity. Without these, we are only high-order animals. Have you ever thought about just what the image of God consists of in us human beings? Obviously it is not our physical shape. Then what? What is it that makes us different from the animals? Oh well, some might say, animals can't reason. I'm not so sure of that! I have encountered some dogs and cows in my time that had remarkable capacities to put one and one together and come up with two. Especially when I didn't want them to!

Well, someone else says, animals aren't self-conscious. How do we know that? Since they can't talk to us it is difficult to be certain. Have you been following the reports of the gorillas that have been taught sign language? Some of the stories are fascinating. For instance, there is the one about the researcher watching from hiding while the gorilla did something it was forbidden to do. Later the researcher asked the gorilla what it had been doing, and the gorilla lied! That takes a pretty high level of awareness.

So what is the image of God? Well, it would be presumptuous for me to suggest that I can solve this age-old problem here. But I do have an idea that one of the elements of that image is the capacity to imagine. What is imagining? The act or power of forming a mental image of something not present to the senses or never before wholly perceived in reality, says *Webster's*. Coupled with this is the ability to give complex expression to what has been imagined. That is creativity, the power to create something, something useful or not useful, but something that has never existed before. So I am saying that we are the most human, the most civilized, when we are the most creative. But there is no true creativity without leisure, the freedom to dream, to imagine, to try.

So whenever we've talked about great civilizations, we've talked about people who are living in some degree of harmony, who are able to stretch and express their imaginations, and who are able to be creative, not simply in terms of ideas, but also in terms of things. And you can't do that if you do not have time to do it. This is why Aristotle says leisure is essential to civilization. There is no civilization without the freedom to look at the world and sort it out—to discover the parts and how they relate to one another.

WHAT IS LEISURE?

A MEANS OR AN END?

This concept of creativity unveils a further element in the Greek idea of leisure. Think about the artist. How does she feel when she can only afford to paint commissioned works? Shut in. We can hear her say, "Well, I've got to earn my bread, so I've got to paint what so-and-so wants." But, oh, how wonderful when she's finally made it! Now she can just express what is within her and not have to feel that she's doing it for pay. Now she feels free—and leisured. Leisure is not the absence of work; it is something more than work.

Work is done for some purpose other than itself. Thus, it is but a means. It is useful; I work in order that I may achieve some other end. But leisure, as the Greeks understood it—and in the light of what it has meant across the centuries—is that which is done for itself. It is an end in itself; it does not have to be useful to some other end. You don't engage in leisure because it's useful.

Now, for many of us, that is a heresy. *Everything* has to be useful—I mean, you don't do it if it's not *good* for something! But leisure is an end in itself. A painting is an end in itself. An essay is an end in itself. I will talk more about this in a later chapter, but let me comment a little further here. Whenever something is done for an end beyond itself, it is very easy for the thing itself not only to become devalued, but to become drudgery. We see this with a great deal of work today. Why should I do this task any better than I have to? After all, the only reason I'm doing this stupid thing is for the paycheck. If all of our lives are filled with activities of this sort, the result is a feeling of entrapment and, worse, dehumanization. But genuine leisure is activity performed for itself alone, and at that point, like the artist, a person is liberated and in that sense of liberation can be lifted once again above the merely animal.

But can't we combine both kinds of activities? Isn't it possible to paint a picture for the sheer joy of it and yet earn money for it, even though that's not the main reason the thing was done? Yes, and that's one of the interesting things in this whole discussion. You see, it is almost impossible for us not to bring leisure—activities performed for themselves alone—into those activities that are performed for some other end.

I remember how, as a teenager plowing, I wanted to get those furrows exactly straight. Why? Yes, my dad had told me that it was a good idea, because once you get a furrow crooked, the next one will be a little more crooked, and before long you're going to have a serious problem. But there's something more than that. There's a special delight in getting that thing ruler straight and being able to look back at the end and say, "Wow!" Why? There is not that much usefulness in a straight furrow. No, I did it for the "fun" of it. I did it for itself alone, and to that extent I was free.

In the same way, think about pottery. A jug is a jug is a jug. But there is something in us human beings that makes the potter want to give that jug an appealing shape and color. Why? It will not hold water any better. It will not be any more useful. Yet somehow making that pot an expression of what the potter sees as beauty becomes an end in itself.

These examples can be duplicated endless times. There is something in us that loves to do things for themselves. But that is not always appreciated in our society. We are a utilitarian culture if ever there was one. If a thing's not useful, it's worthless. So our leisure activities must all serve some other end. It's all right for me to spend five hours reading because I'll work better. It's all right for me to go out on the golf course because I'll live longer. What we have done is to make leisure itself a means. As a result we have lost a part of what the heart of leisure is—the freedom to look at, to appreciate, to understand, to value.

LEISURE AND THE LIBERAL ARTS

This is one of the struggles of our time in education. We have the liberal arts opposed by what we may call the professional arts. Originally these professional arts were called the "servile arts," but that has become a loaded phrase now, for obvious reasons. However, at the outset liberal arts were the opposite of the servile arts. They were the arts that set a person free, while the others only fitted you to find work. Today, few people want a degree in the liberal arts. They say, "The degree is not good for anything. I want a degree that will prepare me to do something. Why read English literature, for heaven's sake? I'm not going to teach it. I'm not going to sell it. I'm not going to write it. So why read it? It's not useful."

But the original idea of the liberal arts was that these are the studies that preview. These are the studies that open up the world to you, which *pre*view. These are the studies that make you able to appreciate and integrate and understand and therefore make you ready to do whatever you need to do elsewhere. Persons with a liberal arts education will be liberated; the ground will have been prepared, and they will be ready to learn the particular job skills that they need over and above the basic life skills. In the sense that the liberal arts prepare you to live, they certainly are "useful." Beyond that, when Aristotle says that leisure is necessary for civilization, he is saying that in a real sense these studies have an ultimate utility. But how easily we mortgage ultimate good for short-term utility.

These thoughts illustrate the difference between work

and leisure. There's an immediate usefulness in work, and there is a broader, more ultimate usefulness in leisure. But do you see what we have done? We have sought to save the liberal arts by arguing for their ultimate utility. We are tempted to save leisure in the same manner. In other words, utility equals value. A thing is valuable if it's useful. Of what value is four hours spent in building a model? It's not useful, so are we to conclude that it's of no value? Or how about an amble through the woods by yourself? Of what use is that? But perhaps value is something more than utility. Nowhere is this more clearly stated than in the Old Testament attitude toward the widow, the orphan, and the stranger. These were persons who had very little usefulness in their society. How easily they could be cast aside on the dump heap of life. But God says, "No, the value of these people, their worth, is not in their contributions. They are not a means to an end. They have value in themselves." Leisure helps us develop this kind of attitude. If we have learned to do things for the sheer enjoyment of them alone, we will be more able to treat people in the same way. So in more ways than one leisure is liberating time.

But along with our tendency to evaluate everything according to its immediate utility, there is another enemy of leisure that is all too common among us. I call it "oughtness." Because we are a driven people in so many ways, there is a subtle hint that creeps into the liberating time contaminating it with the suggestion that we *must* do such and such a thing. I *must* contemplate the world. I *must* sort things out. I *must* see things in relationship. I must, I must. And the whole concept of leisure as freedom goes by the boards. We come again under the tyranny of the imperative. It's as easy to do that with a hobby as with any other activity. Sometimes I find myself as driven to accomplish goals in my hobbies as I am in my work. The "oughtness" creeps back in, and what is to be creative and freeing becomes again tension producing. But this won't be the case if we remember what leisure really is.

LEISURE VERSUS DIVERSION

But without doubt this ideal definition poses problems because most people today have no such idea of leisure. It is time to do what I want. Period. As a result most people have neither the training nor the inclination to use leisure in a civilizing way. And someone has said, probably correctly, that a better term for our non-work time today is "diversion." Thus, we are not seeking leisure time, but rather diversion time, time when our attention can be distracted from whatever it is normally given to.

This concept of leisure as diversion is part of the problem for the Christian church, for when leisure is merely doing what I want, then commitment, discipline, and patience, to name a few qualities, are at a very low premium. Yet these qualities are at the heart of the Christian experience. In fact, they are at the heart of any genuine creativity. For most of us the idea of discipline that gives freedom or of value beyond utility is very difficult to grasp. But if we can implant this broader definition in people's minds, one of the positive by-products will be its effect on Christian commitment.

The picture I've been painting, one that is all too uncommon among us, is of a leisure that is primarily oriented toward mind and spirit. It involves freedom to learn, not so much because learning is useful, but just because it's there and the world is there. It involves an openness to wonder. It involves deliverance from the tyranny of the "ought" into the liberty of the "why not?" It means that instead of becoming less human by escaping into dehumanizing diversions, we become more vitally alive by plunging into the very heart of life. This is leisure as it may be if only we would seize it.

T W O

LEISURE: WHO HAS IT?

In the previous chapter we talked about the new problem facing us in this century—the problem of leisure time. We no longer need to work 80 hours a week to meet our basic needs. But I am going to guess that there is a question going through your mind that we need to deal with before we go a step further. That is the question, "Where is this leisure everybody talks about? If there's so much of it around, why don't I have any?"

I know exactly what you mean. My grandfather farmed with a team of mules. Every fall it took him 10 weeks—from the middle of September until the end of November—to plow and plant 150 acres of winter wheat, and that was working dawn to dusk. But I suspect he was more leisured than I. How can that be? With all of the labor-saving devices at our beck and call, it seems that we ought to have nothing to do. But in fact many of us are run ragged. We are walking evidence of the little motto: "The hurrieder I go, the behinder I get." What's going on here?

Every once in a while I read a book that gives me what I

call an "aha!" experience. Perhaps you've had that kind of experience too. You've thought about something or wondered about something for a long time. Perhaps the thinking or the wondering have been almost subliminal, almost beneath the floor of your conscious mind. Then along comes a book, usually out of the blue, that puts all your thoughts and questions together and comes up with a very plausible answer, and you say, "aha!"

THE HARRIED LEISURE CLASS

I had an experience like that on this question. The book is *The Harried Leisure Class*, by Staffan B. Linder, a Swedish economist who spent some 15 years in America. This unique background on the part of the author allows the book to have a breadth it could not have had otherwise. Linder is able to talk of Western culture in general and not just of Sweden on the one hand or of America on the other. His thesis is deceptively simple: the more we produce, the more we must consume. At this point perhaps someone is suppressing a yawn and saying, "Of course."

But now take the next step: while production may increase by geometrical progression, the amount of time it takes to consume goods is very difficult to reduce. Put another way, Linder is saying that we can't consume a particular item or a particular service much faster than Grandpa could when he really put his mind to consuming. The speed with which an apple pie can be transferred from plate to stomach today shows discouragingly little improvement in speed over the time it took to perform that operation 100 years ago. In my home I have two researchers, ages 12 and 14, who are working on this problem day and night, and there may be a new breakthrough at any moment—but I think you see the point of the argument.

If our society is 100 times more productive than grand-father's was, then we must consume 100 times as many products as he had to, *but in the same amount of time!* No wonder we have so little time! Every waking hour must be spent in the consumption of goods or we will be buried under the enormous output of our Western industrial machine. The alternative is to plunge our fragile economies into a recession, if not a genuine depression, by refusing to buy what is produced.

Undoubtedly this approach to the problem raises a number of questions, but before we can begin to address them, we must consider Linder's analysis in some detail. First of all, consider an example. If by working 10 hours a day I produce—we'll call it 10 units—and if I could consume 5 units in 2 hours, my total time for the day is 10 hours spent in production plus 2 hours spent in consumption, or 12 hours total. In the remaining 12 hours of my day, I am free to do whatever I would like. But now suppose I become so much more productive that in 8 hours I can produce 40 units. Now it is going to take me 8 hours to consume what I have produced (or the equivalent that someone else has produced, assuming that the society as a whole is roughly as productive as I). Those 8 hours plus the 8 I spend producing total 16 hours. Thus, though I am *working* 2 fewer hours, I actually have 4 fewer hours to call my own. Who says we have more time?

FIVE USES OF TIME

Linder divides time into five areas. The first is specialized production time, the time when you are producing goods or services. It would be what we would call a person's "job." This does not have to be remunerated work, so long as it is an occupation that produces goods and services. Thus, homemaking involves specialized production time. (By the way, notice that in English, material things are called "goods." Isn't that interesting? Things are *good*! That is certainly true biblically. This is a good world. But things are not the ultimate goal, as our society seems to be in danger of coming to believe. "Goods" are not good in and of themselves.)

The second block of time is personal work time. Those of us raised in the fundamentalist or evangelical subcultures may be thinking of Christian witnessing here, but I assure you, this is not what Linder has in mind! Rather, this is the maintenance of our bodies and possessions. To give a ludicrous example, one of the things my grandfather didn't have to spend any time on was putting on deodorant. Now we produce it by the tons, by the thousands of tons, and we use it. Not, I hasten to add, merely for economic reasons! However, the first fellow who began to produce deodorant undoubtedly had to create a popular desire for his product. At any rate, the more personal care products there are and the more possessions I have, the more personal work time is going to be expended in the maintenance of my body and possessions. Now take the lawn, for instance. The lawn is a possession. Actually, I'm not sure whether it possesses me or I possess it! Anyway, I have to have a seeder, a mower, and a roller, and a tractor to pull the seeder, the mower, and the roller. Then I have to find the time to put this whole menagerie through its paces! That's personal work time.

The third block of time is consumption time. This is the time when we are actually using goods or services. This may be for recreation or for other purposes, but its central focus is on consumption. In a highly productive society, more and more ways must be found to bring consumption into every phase of life. For instance, simply taking a brisk walk in a baggy sweater, patched jeans, and holey sneakers will not do. To exercise "properly," one must be decked out in a matched warm-up suit with a prestigious name on it and a pair of hundred-dollar, computer-designed running shoes. Consumption is the name of the game.

Linder's fourth category is time for the cultivation of mind and spirit. This time may use some goods and services, but consumption is not the major focus. Conversation with a friend would be a good example of this kind of time. So would a visit to a museum. Likewise personal devotions or participation in a worship service.

The fifth category is idleness—doing absolutely nothing. As Linder says, probably the only truly idle people in the world are the desperately poor who produce so little that they consume it at once. In a highly productive society idleness is almost impossible to come by. Instead the demands on our time increase to the point where there is no room for one thing more. In freeway terminology, we have experienced gridlock; so many vehicles have entered the highway that none can move to the point of exit. Some of us are at mental and emotional gridlock.

WHAT CAN WE DO?

So, someone says, let's just quit consuming. Unfortunately, it's not quite so simple. First, there are the social and economic reasons. Given our high productivity, we *must* purchase and consume one another's goods. If we do not, then masses of us are going to be unemployed. For in fact a small percentage of our total work force can now produce what is necessary to meet the basic needs of our whole society. This is a part of what is happening on our farms. American farmers are the most productive farmers the world has ever seen. They are so productive, in fact, that the rest of us cannot eat fast enough to consume all that they are producing. The result? Steadily falling prices for farm commodities; massive government stockpiles of unwanted food; farm bankruptcies and human misery.

What are our options if we are too productive, then? We cannot each become less productive, because then we cannot make enough money to live on. Neither can we very easily select some people not to produce, though some would argue that that is the net effect of the welfare state. All that is left to us is to find more sophisticated and compelling ways to encourage, nay, coerce, people into consuming more. I am a fine example of the success of this effort. My day has simply not started if I do not have a glass of orange juice. If coffee is "Swedish gasoline" to get the Swede started on his or her day, orange juice is mine. Why do I have to have orange juice? Because of advertising. The success of the citrus industry in this country is the result of an advertising triumph. At the turn of the century, with improved strains and better yields, the citrus growers realized that they had to find some way of increasing the demand for their product. Given a highly efficient rail system that also needed to market its product, it was apparent that the key was to create a desire for orange juice in the East. That I, 85 years later, feel deprived if I don't have orange juice with my breakfast is a testimony both to the success of the original campaign and also to the success of the continuing one.

THE GRATIFICATION CURVE

But not only are there social and economic reasons why it is not easy to limit consumption, there are also personal ones. For instance, we have an ingrained aversion to "waste." Something says, "If I made it, I ought to use it. If it's there, it ought not to be wasted." But beyond that there is a chilling phenomenon called the law of diminishing returns. Initially many pleasures can be enhanced with more goods. For instance, if you have a cheap phonograph, your pleasure can be intensified by getting an $800 one. But what do you do then? If you spend $2,500 on a really first-class system, it increases your pleasure further, but not by the same amount as that $800 unit did. In Linder's terms the gratification curve levels off.

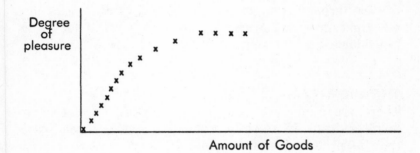

So what do you do now? Do you say, well, since that $2,500 system did not give me three times as much pleasure as the $800 one, I'll just sell the expensive one and go back to the $800 version. Not very likely. What is more likely is that you will end up spending six or seven times *more* money on a new system in a vain attempt to duplicate that first pleasure increase. We must work even more hours in order to pay for these greatly increased goods. What we have is all too similar to a heroin addiction—there always has to be a bigger fix.

In this regard Linder makes the very interesting observation that when all factors (moonlighting, overtime, part-time work, etc.) are considered, the actual per capita workload has not decreased any since World War II. Total production time is still, according to his calculations, around 48 hours a week. Why? Because people believe they have to work more to achieve the possessions they believe are essential to their well-being. So then, just because we don't *have* to work 50 hours a week doesn't mean we won't. In fact, when steelworkers were granted 37-hour weeks, many reported that they especially liked the reduction because it gave them a chance to get a second job. So we find ourselves on a treadmill: the more we produce, the more we must consume, but the more we consume, the more we feel we need to earn through production. In many ways it appears that economic growth has become an end in itself for us as individuals and for the society as a whole.

THE HIGH COST OF SERVICE

There are a number of other disquieting corollaries to Linder's thesis. In a highly productive society it takes less time to produce something new than it does to service something used. If I am so productive that I can produce a new car in the time that it takes you to service an old one, we become a throw-away culture. It is no longer a "cost-efficient" use of time to service the old car. Since time is the one absolutely fixed commodity we have, time becomes increasingly precious. This means that when service cannot be avoided, it will be almost prohibitively costly. As a result we are forced to discard an otherwise good item for want of a relatively simple repair. You or I could probably perform the repair ourselves, but then we don't have the time either.

Even more disturbing in this kind of society where production time is cheaper than service time, is the fact that those who depend most on services are those most in need. Who are the people who most need service? The elderly and the very young. What are we going to do when Grandma gets ill and needs around-the-clock care? It does not make good economic sense for one person—or two—to take care of one other person when time is so valuable. What to do? You put all the grandmas and grandpas together in a nursing home, where one adult can now service 20 people at the same time. Personal attention? Oh, well, they'll get along.

We put children in a day-care facility. Instead of one adult servicing 2 or 3 children, now one adult services 10 to 20 children. Why have we done this? Because Mother can make more money—she can use her time more productively—in production than in service. Her time will be of greater monetary value to the family if she's at work and some lower-skilled person is being paid to take care of 10 to 12 children.

This last point brings out another facet of the matter. Not only will service be very expensive in this kind of setting, but frequently it will be poor because the only reason the person is in the service sector is because he or she is not qualified for a more lucrative production position.

Yet another element in the picture is that it is cheaper to produce exotic medicines and complex health machinery than it is to get nurses. What are we short of in our society? We're not short of $250,000 CAT-scan machines. We have them; what we don't have are nurses. Moreover, it is hard to get them at any price because generally production is much less taxing than service.

Another one of these disquieting corollaries is this—less and less time will be devoted to decisions. If production time is cheaper than decision time, it is inefficient to spend much time on decisions. Let me see if I can illustrate. If you and your spouse together make $150 dollars a day, it would be foolish for the two of you to take two or three days off from work to do comparison shopping on a new car in order to save a few hundred dollars. Moreover, if your time demands are already at gridlock, you don't have the time to give to the decision even if you wanted to. What to do? Make the most informed decision you can in the minimum amount of time and hope that if it's a bad one, you can make enough money in production to offset the decision's effects. Not only is this characteristic of individuals in a productive society, says Linder, it is even more true of governments. Because decision time is so costly, again and again governments jump for the quick fix. But on this level bad decisions, as most recently on the Sgt. York gun, can be horrendously expensive, and bad political decisions can be disastrous.

CONSUME MORE!

Another implication of this situation is that if consumption time is limited, which it surely is, but consumable goods are rapidly increasing, we must find ways to maximize our consumption time. How do we do that? We have to consume more goods per unit of time. This means that we must spend less time on a greater number of goods. We must devote less and less time to any one of our possessions in order to give more time to the total. We will enjoy each possession less and less and may even enjoy the aggregate less because of frustration with our limited time.

Another way to maximize consumption is to give precedence to activities that stress consumption over those that do not. There goes leisure as we described it in the previous chapter! Now we must use our free time to spend money. Linder was writing in 1970. At that time he predicted that if his hypothesis was correct, those activities that take a great deal of time but do not consume many goods would diminish. Unfortunately, he said, building an enduring love relationship is terribly time-consuming. Thus he suspected that long-lasting love affairs were likely to decrease and one-night stands were likely to increase.

Likewise, cultural pursuits tend to be time-intensive rather than goods-intensive. In Linder's view this makes them an endangered species. Given the amount of time that must be spent in consumption, there will be precious little left over for thinking, dreaming, imagining, and appreciating. No longer may anything be enjoyed merely for itself. It must provide a means to the greater end: consumption, and beyond that, economic growth.

The conditions Linder foresaw as probable in 1970 have come true. Our productivity is killing us, and it is killing true leisure. Conspicuous, obsessive consumption has nothing to do with that civilizing reflection upon and exploration of life that the Greeks envisioned for their free time. There will be no easy solutions to this problem, but we must do our best to find them. Jesus' words are still true, "A man's real life in no way depends upon the number of his possessions" (Luke 12:15, PH).

Let me close with a story from another author, very much in the same spirit. A fellow dreamed that he woke up in A.D. 2100 and found a man living with his family in a huge, palatial house. Each morning this man got up early, wolfed down his breakfast, and rushed off to work. His "work" was spending a certain amount of ration stamps. He had a quota that he had to spend every day. If he didn't meet his quota by the end of the week, he was issued a larger quota for the next week. When he came home in the evening, harried from trying to spend all of these stamps, his wife would nag at him because they had to live in the slums. You see, the poorest people lived in the biggest houses. The more elite you were, the smaller the house you had. The really elite were permitted to live in a bungalow. They didn't have to spend anything—and they could even have gardens.

T H R E E

THE LEISURE GUILT TRIP

So far we've talked about two basic questions concerning leisure: what it means ideally and why we have so little of it. In this chapter I want to deal with a third basic question: If leisure is such a good thing, why do I feel so guilty when I'm engaged in it?

Now maybe this is not a problem for all of us, but in the circles in which I move, I know of very few people who don't have to force themselves to take time off. Beyond that, when they do take time off, many of them are uneasy if the "off" time is not pretty well filled. Why should that be? And why is this guilt as pervasive as it seems to be?

WE NEED TO BE USEFUL

I think our attitudes are at the center of the problem. Let me use my father as an example. He grew up on a farm and worked there full time until I was born. When I was born to my mother and dad, he was 45. Coming in addition to two sisters, I imposed just enough of an additional financial burden that he decided to get a job in a brass foundry in a nearby city. But he didn't sell the farm. As long as he was employed at the foundry, he worked two jobs—eight hours there and then another eight or ten on the farm.

That was my father's life until he was 70, when he was forcibly retired from the foundry. By that time he and mother had left the farm. Two weeks after he retired he had a relatively minor hernia operation; he very nearly died from that operation. He said afterward, "I just thought to myself, 'I'm useless. Why go on living?'"

Fortunately for him, and us, my uncle, my mother's brother, who was the manager of an estate nearby, needed a yardman that spring and hired my father. That got him through that year. The next spring the yard job opened up again and about a month later, around the first of June, my cousin, who runs a 400-acre dairy farm, had a hired hand quit without notice. He asked my dad if he could help out temporarily. That was 18 years ago.

Ever since then my dad has managed to make it through the winter, but from about the first of April until the end of November he works eight hours on the estate, mowing lawns, trimming grass, cutting down trees, and so on. Then he jumps into his car, which for about 15 years was a flaming yellow VW, and drives 14 miles out in the country and works until sundown on my cousin's farm. Since the VW died and went to that place reserved for all faithful Bugs, he has gotten a somewhat more sedate car—but not much! And the routine continues uninterrupted. At dark he comes home and falls into bed anticipating tomorrow.

My uncle retired several years ago, but Daddy stays on. This past fall, for his 90th birthday, the owners of the estate bought a luxurious new lawn tractor for him! No wonder! They would have a hard time ever finding anyone else as conscientious as he. You see, he doesn't work for money, but to live. That's what he has needed in order to go on living: to be useful.

One Christmas vacation I sat typing a learned paper at the kitchen table in my folk's home. I started about 7:30 in the morning. My dad left to go to work with my cousin, and when he came home at about 5:00, I was still sitting at the table typing. He looked at me and sort of chuckled, or maybe "snorted" is closer, and said, "I want to know which of us was performing the most useful work today. I was hauling manure. How about you? I'm feeding the world. What are you doing?" Well, knowing the topic of that paper, it may be that hauling manure was more valuable!

My father is a wonderful person whom I would not change for the world, but his story illustrates a certain attitude toward life. According to this attitude, unless what we do has immediate utility, we are not contributing. Unless you are doing something useful in immediate terms, you are idle, slothful, which is a biblical sin. In this light, as I suggested earlier, recreation is only of value if it makes you more efficient; the only purpose for playing is that you will be more productive. So if your play doesn't seem to make you more productive, you ought not to be playing. If I can't show my boss that improving my golf game really is necessary in order to make that big sale on the links someday, or that my reading will make me a better conversationalist, then I ought not to be doing those things. So goes this line of thought.

I AM WHAT I DO

According to these attitudes, a person *is* what he or she does. We are not persons of value in ourselves. We are persons of value because we do something, because we produce something. While many of the aims and results of the contemporary women's movement are good, I have a deep nagging fear that in fact many women are falling into the trap that we men have been in for a long time, the idea that you are of value because you *do* something. You are of value because you produce something. To that extent, it seems to me that the women's liberation movement will not produce liberation, but only a different kind of slavery, a slavery to producing more in order to be worth more.

This attitude cannot help but make us feel guilty about doing something other than work. I am what I do. I am now a teacher, so if I am not teaching, what am I? Who am I? It is much easier to fill every moment with "useful" occupations and feel harried and driven than it is to have unanswered questions about my self-worth.

Where do these attitudes come from? I think that three of the most important sources for them are racial memory, the influence of Scripture, and what has come to be called the Protestant work ethic.

Racial memory. This is a concept proposed by the psychologists Adler and Jung. It suggests that the genes and chromosomes carry information not only about our physical, mental, and emotional makeup, but also about ideas and attitudes that millennia of human experience have imprinted there. (Personally, I find this the only satisfactory explanation for the transmission of original sin.)

Through most of the history of human experience every hand had to pitch in or we'd starve. So I think the whole idea that only what is immediately useful is of value has been imprinted on our very memories. This is the point of Aesop's classic fable of the grasshopper. He wanted to play the violin all summer while the ants collected food. But in the winter when it began to snow and he wanted some food, the ants said, "No. You didn't help." That's been part of human life for most of the time we've been here on this planet. Those who don't work don't eat. The impact of several millennia of that experience upon us has left its mark. So I think this racial memory partly accounts for the attitudes that make us feel guilty about leisure.

The influence of Scripture. A second cause for these attitudes is biblical material. I just want to touch on this now since we will look at it in more detail later in the book. There can be no doubt that the Scripture speaks clearly on the value of work and on the disvalue of idleness or sloth. Proverbs is a favorite source for sermons on labor and the value of work. One example is Proverbs 10:4-5: "A slack hand causes poverty, but the hand of the diligent makes rich. A son who gathers in summer is prudent, but a son who sleeps in harvest brings shame" (RSV). That's before Aesop. There are biblical reinforcements to the idea that it is good to work and bad not to work.

The Protestant work ethic. Thirdly, and I think probably most significantly, our guilt is a part of our religious heritage. This can be traced to the Reformation. The Roman Catholic Church divided sacred and secular work. It said that the work, or the product, of the monk or the nun was of greater value than the work of the lay brother or sister. The really necessary activity in life was religious contemplation. That was important.

I'll never forget when that understanding of priorities came home to me. As a part of one of our classes in seminary we went to visit a nearby Trappist monastery. The Trappists are a part of the order Bernard of Clairvaux founded and are among the most ascetic of monks. One of their rigors is a vow of silence.

The Guest Master who had been granted a special dispensation to speak to us and who so cordially escorted us was a big, strapping, blond fellow who looked as if he'd just gotten out of a football uniform or walked off a movie set.

We were with him for two or three hours, and finally one of us felt we knew him well enough to ask him the question we'd all been wanting to ask from the beginning. The question was, although my fellow student put it more tactfully than this, "What in the world is a talented, good-looking guy like you doing here?"

I'll never forget how shocked I was when that vibrant young man responded, "I thought about my life and thought that probably the most helpful thing I could do for the world was to pray for it." I don't know how that hit the rest of my classmates, but it hit me right in the pit of the stomach. You see, for me, really "useful" ministry was preaching, or street witnessing, or counseling, or Christian education, or—you know—*work!* The thought that a life of contemplation, worship, and prayer could be the most valuable ministry of all was stunning.

So, for the Roman Catholic Church work for God was a vocation and other work was just work. To be sure, that other work was important in God's sight, but it was not as important as a churchly vocation.

When the Reformation came, the situation changed. Just as the priesthood of all believers meant that all believers had immediate access to God, so also it meant that all work is sacred, an expression of each person's divine calling. Whatever you did, that was your contribution to God. If you were a milker of cows, then that was your divine calling. God had intended for you to be a milker of cows.

The next step is an easy one. Since God decreed your job for you, it is plain that your life is your job. Your life is cow milking. Your significance on this planet is wrapped up in cow milking, and you are intended by God to find your contentment and your identity in cow milking.

Most writers, both Christian and non-Christian, agree that this attitude formed the essential foundation for the industrial revolution. Production is not merely what one does to maintain physical life. Rather it is a sacrament, a fulfillment of one's eternal destiny. Thus, material production becomes a divine calling. You live out your life before God by producing.

This then accounts for the Puritan attitude. You don't have time to make jokes. Your calling and the living out of your calling are too serious to fuss around with funnies. Put that together with frugality and prudence, and you have what has been called the Protestant, or Puritan, work ethic. Nor are we talking of a merely Lutheran or Calvinist sentiment here, for we have these words of John Wesley, "Leisure and I have parted company. I am resolved to be busy until I die." We are looking at the spirit of an age.

Before I go further here, I should not leave the impression that our spiritual fathers were stern, humorless drudges. The stories of Luther's playfulness abound, and it is reported of Wesley that he was one of the best storytellers you could find, able to entertain company for hours at a stretch with one story after another. I'm not sure how he justified that occupation. Surely it wasn't leisure!

At any rate, Wesley's original statement is very much out of his own milieu. Who am I? I am Wesley; I am called to reform this continent. That's me. That's my calling. And I must labor at that calling every moment or I will displease God.

This attitude was easily transported to America where it was necessary to work 20 hours a day to keep out the howling wilderness. Add the Puritan heritage of the New England states and the religious fervor of the revivals of the late 1700s and early 1800s and you have no difficulty understanding what has been called America's religious marching song, "Work, for the Night Is Coming." If your experience is like mine, you haven't sung that very recently. But I remember that our church sang it pretty regularly when I was a child. I also remember that I used to wonder, if the night was coming and we could stop working then, why we didn't just stop working now and be done with it. Why not just sit down and wait for the night to come? But I didn't say that to anybody. Although I didn't know just why, I sensed that it would not be appreciated. Somehow I knew that, whatever the reason, you were *supposed* to work.

Although we may not sing that song so much anymore, that religious heritage is still applicable for most of us, especially those of us who grew up in the fundamentalist or evangelical traditions. Most of us I think tend to see our particular vocation as our calling, as our identity, as our nature. Who am I? I am a professor at a seminary. What must I do to fulfill that calling? Well, it means that I must have my students on my mind every waking hour. Even if I am not actually teaching or preparing for classes, I ought to be thinking about it. How can I justify doing anything else when the task is of such cosmic importance? Who am I if I am not teaching? That is my identity before God. To engage in any other kind of activity is to be no one.

While this religiously based concept still holds true for many of us, what about that mass of people around us for whom organized religion no longer holds any significance? Many of them still feel guilty about leisure. What has happened is this: with the loss of the religious underpinning, work itself has become the substitute for devotion. Before, we worked as an expression of our devotion to God; we worked as an attempt to fulfill our divine callings. But as that religious underpinning slowly eroded, work itself became the end rather than the means. It became its own reason and its own reward. You get some feel for that when you look at the semireligious nature of the early granger organizations and labor unions. I no longer work for God; I work for Labor itself.

But as labor has become less and less meaningful, such a position has become harder and harder to sell. You work because work is its own reward: tell that to a guy who spends all day putting left-handed nuts on bolts, and if he doesn't punch you out, he will at least say, "Come on, tell me another one. What's the value of this, what's the utility of it, what's the good of it? Where's my pride of accomplishment at the end of a day? Beat it!"

Now this situation brings us to a crossroads. We could say that work *is* just a means to an end and of no particular value in itself, or we could try to find some other way to sanctify work (and produce guilt over leisure in another way). Marxism is an example of this second way. Interestingly enough, Harvey Cox in his book *Feast of Fools* puts Luther and Marx together in this matter. I'm not sure either of them would like that very well. Nevertheless, Cox says that for both Luther and Marx working is the meaning of life. But Marx, having lost the divine dimension, must find another way to give work, especially industrial work, that kind of dignity. His answer was to put the worker in control of the means of production. In other words, the worker will decide what is to be produced and when and where and how it is to be produced. The worker will decide these matters, not the capitalist, not the boss. In this way Marx expected to enable the worker to feel as though he or she had control over his or her destiny. Now instead of being merely a drone, the worker can be a contributor to social progress. Now instead of working for the capitalist's God, we work for society.

There is much about this theory that is noble, but as the experiment has shown in the Soviet Union, Marx did not really take into account original sin. Human ideals tend to get lost very quickly if there is not a check on our inbred rapacity. In addition, impersonal society is not an adequate replacement for the personal, caring God. Why should I work for an abstraction that neither knows I exist nor cares?

In North America, where socialist theory has not yet gained full sway, work has become primarily a means to money, and money has value because it is supposedly a means to freedom. I work. Why? Because it's valuable? No, I work to get money. Why? Because I want money for itself? Well, not particularly. What I really believe is that money will buy me the ability to do whatever I want. But this becomes a will-o'-the-wisp that in fact leads me in circles. The money doesn't procure as much freedom as I thought; therefore, I'll go back to work in order to get more money to get more freedom.

Our religious heritage, which enthroned work as the very essence of one's being, has decayed. It has decayed into Marxism in much of the world, while here in the West it has decayed into the thirst for freedom and well-being by means of money. Nevertheless, work is still seen as the means to whatever matters in life.

WORKING TO AVOID LEISURE

Thus far I have given three reasons why I think we feel guilty about leisure time. The first was racial memory: the instinctive sense that we must work constantly in order to survive. The second reason was biblical: certain biblical statements teach us the value of work. The third reason was our religious heritage: it is in work that we fulfill our destiny as human beings.

I think there is at least one more reason for our sense of guilt over leisure, and that is our lack of ability to capitalize on leisure. The French essayist and thinker Baudelaire wrote these frightening words: "One must work, if not from taste, then at least from despair, for to reduce everything to a single truth, work is less boring than pleasure." I think there are a lot of people in our society who are discovering this same truth and who indeed go to work because it's less boring than pleasure.

Why should this be so? I suggested in chapter 1 that we are not taught how to contemplate or how to appreciate. If the true value of leisure is in our ability to look at the world, to be free to look at it and to receive from it its meaning and its value, and we can't do that, then we've got a problem. We are not able to be creative, many of us. We've not been taught—and though I use the word *taught*, for want of a better one, I am not intending to imply that the defect is merely the fault of our teachers—to become creative. Part of the reason for this is the curse of utility. Don't try to create something, because it probably won't be good for anything. So you have a woodworking shop—well, how many bookcases can you get rid of? Production and utility. We have not been educated for living but for working, under the false belief that working *is* living.

Think about the nature of your own education and your attitudes toward it. What is education? Education is not a means to live. It is a series of courses to be passed in order to obtain a diploma with which you can then go to work. But what if education was the unfolding of a world to be explored? What if education was the opening of possibilities? The painting of vistas? Exposure to ideas? Then education in a real sense would not be a means to an end; in a real sense it would become an end in itself. It would be a part of the development of human beings. That it is seldom these things is in part the fault of us teachers. It's easier to teach a syllabus than it is to open minds to ideas.

The fundamentals cannot be ignored, though. Until we have mastered basic skills and facts, we have no foundation on which to rest ideas and vistas and possibilities. So we can't just sail right over the basics in order to get to "truly meaningful" education. What we can do is teach even the basics from the point of view of discovery. Then perhaps more of us would see education not merely as something to be gotten through, but as something to be gotten into.

So then, because we are not prepared to take advantage of leisure, our free time becomes filled with diversions that are both increasingly addictive and increasingly boring. That is a strange duality. The more football I watch, the more I want to watch. And yet at the same time, when you've seen one football game, you've seen them all. So, though I simply *must* see the next game, in a real sense I have already seen it. Increasing addiction and increasing boredom. These are the twin results when our nonworking time is filled with diversion instead of leisure. What then? That inner compass of the human soul that is constantly weighing and measuring, sorting gold from tin, says, "Buddy, there oughta be something better than this," and we feel guilty. Whether you call it conscience or not, we have an instinctive sense of what is less than the best. Since most of what passes for leisure among us is not constructive, but destructive, that sense tells us, "You shouldn't be doing this." Unfortunately that sense tends not to discriminate within categories very well. It tends to condemn whole areas of behavior, even when some of it may be deeply wholesome.

WHAT CAN WE DO?

So I think there are at least four reasons why we feel guilty about leisure: the racial one, the biblical one, the religious-cultural one, and the value one. Of the four, the first is both the easiest to dismiss and, perhaps, the hardest to get rid of, because it is so deeply ingrained. But the plain fact is that it is *not* any longer necessary to work every hour of the day. Knowing this may not make the guilt feelings go away, but we can at least deal with them in a rational way.

The second and third reasons demand a fuller treatment, and that will be the focus of the next section of this book. What *does* the Bible say about work and leisure anyway? What *is* the meaning of work for a Christian and, indeed, for everyone?

The last reason will be addressed in the final section. What can we do to recapture for ourselves the real meaning and value of leisure? If we can answer that question effectively, then we begin to answer our consciences and to reprogram them to recognize that leisure is not tin but gold.

PART TWO
GOD'S VIEW OF WORK

F O U R

WHY DO WE WORK?

We have dealt with three preliminary, but crucial, questions. All of them relate to a proper understanding of what leisure can be. We need to see its potential for humanizing us. We need to free it from a bondage to goods. We need to be able to put it in a right relationship to job and work. With these in mind we are now ready to ask the most important question of all: what does the Bible have to say about leisure? This question is of utmost importance because it is only through the revealed Scriptures that we can ever hope to find our way through the tangled undergrowth of modern culture.

However, the superficial answer to our question is disappointing. There is no place in the Bible where leisure is specifically discussed. In no place does the Bible say that you shall do this with your leisure time and you shall not do that or that you may spend this many hours doing this and this many doing that. No, there is nothing of this sort. But when you think of it, it's not hard to understand why there should be no such passage. As I said in the beginning, we're the first people ever to have much time when we don't have to work in order to meet basic needs. So if the Lord in His wisdom had caused someone to put a statement in the Bible on the Christian use of leisure time, you can imagine how a Moses would have reacted: "Lord, what are You talking about?"

This is the same reason there's nothing in the Bible on the proper use of automobiles or cigarettes, though if you take a particular stance on the interpretation of prophecy, you may want to assert that Ezekiel has something on helicopters! But whatever your position, it is evident that we must do the same with leisure as with automobiles and cigarettes: we must look for larger principles that may be applied to the contemporary issue.

When we look for those larger principles, the first thing that becomes clear is that the Bible contains a number of specific statements about the nature of work. If we study these, we will lay the necessary foundation for the more general teachings that relate to leisure. There are eight of these statements on work. I have arranged them into three groups. The first group deals with the question posed in the title of this chapter.

SUBDUE THE EARTH
At the very outset of the Bible and of human experience we have the command, "subdue the earth." Now maybe before the fall of the human race subduing the earth wasn't hard labor. I don't know about that, but it surely was a task, a goal. God didn't say, "Adam, Eve, enjoy." He said, "Adam, Eve, subdue."

Now what does this idea of subduing the earth contain? As I have just suggested, it must certainly carry with it the idea of responsibility, task, goals. Human beings have a function beyond mere existence. We are to bring the natural realm into order. This is the responsibility that has been given to us. It is probably going too far to say that this is the reason we were brought into existence. But, having been brought into existence, this is the task the Father assigned to us immediately.

This commandment has a number of implications. For instance, it shows us that human beings are not merely part of the natural realm, as the Eastern religions and as many modern followers of the philosophy of naturalism would hold. Humanity stands over the natural realm and has a responsibility for it.

There are those who say that this biblical teaching is responsible for our present ecological problems, suggesting that if we felt more a part of nature and did not have the right to subdue it to our will, some of the despoiling that has occurred in the last couple of centuries would not have taken place. However, it does not take a great deal of thought to refute such a position. In the first place, whenever human beings have had the ability, whatever their religious position, they have sought to bring a nature that they considered hostile to them under control. Second, the Hindu religion, which would most clearly promote oneness among all things, has not produced a model of harmony between human beings and nature but has created a fatalism that has blandly accepted disease and pollution as part of the given world. Finally, the biblical command to subdue the earth is not a license to do whatever we want with it, but it is a charge to accept responsibility for its cultivation and the realization of its possibilities. This idea is strengthened by the Old Testament idea of the land as belonging to God. No family owned its land outright but rather held it as a trust from God. Therefore, no member of the family had the right to sell his or her land to someone outside the family. Furthermore, mistreatment of God's land could very well result in eviction (2 Chron. 36:20-21).

This concept of subduing the earth as responsibility is seen in the relation of the word *subdue* to kingship. A king is to subdue his kingdom; that is, he is to bring it under control and in so doing maximize its potential. What this does *not* mean is that the king has the right to exploit his kingdom for his own benefit. The king is considered to be the shepherd of his kingdom, and the one who exploits the flock, devouring and destroying it for his own gain, is not fit to be king.

A PURPOSE FOR WORK

What this concept of subduing the earth does for the idea of work is to give it its proper context. Why do we work? In order to bring the earth to its true potential. We do not work merely to keep body and soul together, nor do we work just to make some money. We work in order to make the earth more nearly all that it can be. Work in and of itself is not necessarily good or bad. The question is whether my work is achieving this goal that God has set for the human race.

If leisure is the freedom to contemplate the world and to come to a deeper understanding of the world, work cannot achieve its real purposes without leisure. Until we understand the true nature of the earth, there is no possibility of our effective exercise of that benevolent sovereignty over the world that God intends for us to have.

If our work involves the idea of kingship, this implies something else. While the king has the task, the responsibility, the work, he also has the right of enjoyment. Thus, none of us is intended to be merely a cog in the machine. We are, as kings and queens, those who have the right of privilege and enjoyment in that task.

WORK'S THORNS AND THISTLES

This fairly lofty idea of the nature and purpose of work is, like everything else, contaminated by the fall of humanity into sin. Whatever work might have been if Adam and Eve had not sinned, it is very clear that the Bible has no rose-colored view of work since the Fall.

This is one of the reasons I am convinced that the Bible is from God: it is so wonderfully realistic. Leave it to the writers of popular brochures to speak of the nobility of labor and the uplifting qualities of honest work. The Bible says that work is going to be hard and often frustrating. God tells Adam that he will work by the sweat of his brow—it's going to be hard. There will be thistles and briars to contend with—it's going to be frustrating.

So much for the glorious human laborer. There's not much glory in thorns and thistles. There's not much glory in the sweat running down your face and getting in your eyes and stinging or in feeling like your back's going to break. The Bible does not depict work as the ideal way to find fulfillment and satisfaction. Necessary, yes: we *will* work. But it is not in work that any of us will find absolute fulfillment.

By the same token, just as no man will find complete fulfillment in work, neither will any woman find complete fulfillment in a husband and childbearing. Yes, she'll be attracted to it, she'll be drawn to it, but she won't find ultimate fulfillment in it. Childbearing (and child rearing) will always be painful; relations with a husband will always fall short of what she dreams of.

Now something needs to be pointed out here. This passage in Genesis 3 has been given a great deal of attention in recent years as we have sought to achieve genuine equality between the sexes. On the one hand, there have been those who have insisted that this account makes it clear that God has decreed that men shall work outside the home while women, in submission to men, bear children and make a home. Others have insisted that that kind of role distinction, while it may reflect conditions in the fallen human race in general, has no relevance for Christians because Christ has come to do away with sin.

But the passage nowhere says that men *must* work or that women *must* make a home. Rather, it describes the conditions under which labor and homemaking will occur. And, so far as I can see, those conditions still apply, even among Christians. We still experience struggle and difficulty in all areas of our lives. To be sure, the presence of Christ and the confidence of eternal life to come mitigates these to a significant extent, but they are there nevertheless.

Work itself is not the curse, nor is homemaking; rather, the curse is the conditions under which these occur. But why does the Bible relate labor to men and homemaking to women, if these are not directives? I think the Scriptures are speaking descriptively and not proscriptively here. God is saying that in that place where each of us would most easily find fulfillment, we will instead find frustration. Men *do* most easily find fulfillment in a task and women *do* most easily find fulfillment in the home. This is not to say that all *must* find their fulfillment in these ways, or that something is wrong with them if they don't. But it does talk about usual patterns reflecting who we are, and if we encourage people to ignore these patterns, we invite them to increased frustration.

But why does God do this to His children? Is this just an expression of arbitrary pique because they disobeyed a command of His? No. In fact, this curse is a blessing. It ensures that we will never be able to miss that final bliss for which we have been created merely because we found fulfillment in something else. If we could find total satisfaction in our work or in our homes, we would never know we needed God, never sense that something was missing in our lives, and drop over the brink into hell all unknowing. As it is, all people on earth meet with struggle and frustration in every part of their lives, and if they will listen, God speaks and offers Himself as the source of that total fulfillment for which they long.

Yes, the task of subduing the earth is ours, given to men and women alike. It is a task of noble proportions and demanding possibilities. It means that all work, any work, has great potential. But work, in and of itself, is not divine. In fact, work will be a source of struggle and frustration. It is God for whom we seek, and work is just one limited component of the search.

A DAY NOT TO WORK

A third specific statement of the Bible relating to work is the fourth commandment (Ex. 20:8). There are six days for work, but there is one day when work is not permitted. Why not? Because our lives do not depend on our work. How easily we come to believe that it is our strength or our cleverness or our diligence that accounts for what we have and are! But in fact nothing we have is ours. All we have are gifts: our health, our abilities, our time, and our opportunities are all gifts from God. So every week we set one day aside to remind ourselves that we do not supply our needs, but God does, and to thank Him for His supply.

There is a deeper meaning to the biblical teaching on the Sabbath than the mere prohibition of work. It is the glorious freedom *from* work. On the seventh day God rested and said, "That is the special day, the holy day, the day away from work." *Not* working is special. The Book of Hebrews picks up this same theme when it speaks of the rest that is to be—when we have ceased from our labors and have received God's grace. What this says is that there is nothing intrinsically valuable about work. Rest is just as important as work, and in some ways it is more important, for work gives way to rest. This is Sunday, the day when with a sigh of relief I can recall that my life is not my responsibility, but God's gift. Furthermore, no one can require me to work on this day. Rest is my right.

A DAY TO CELEBRATE

We have said that the Sabbath is a holy day, that is, a holiday. For most of us *holiday* means something other than the "day of prohibitions" that Sunday at least used to mean. Where did the idea of celebration, which is now central to our idea of holiday, come to be attached to "holy day"?

Actually the idea of celebration is at the heart of both the Jewish Sabbath and the Christian Lord's Day. Some of the attempts to inject festivity into worship are more than a little mawkish, since celebration is not merely balloons and dancing in the streets. However, the idea itself is not a bad one, for the Sabbath is a time of joy, a day to reflect on and delight in the fact that your identity does not rest in what you have accomplished, but in who you are in God.

The Scriptures discuss this significance of the Sabbath in two ways. First, there is rejoicing because of a relationship—we can rest because we belong to God, who rested. We are not our own, nor do we belong to our employers. We are God's. So the Sabbath is a holiday because it's an opportunity to celebrate who we are.

But it's also celebration of a standing. This is particularly seen in the version of the Ten Commandments given in Deuteronomy (5:12-15). Why do you rest? Because you're not slaves anymore. Why do you rest? In celebration of your freedom.

What is Christianity about? It's about a relationship; it's about a standing; it's about freedom. And that's what the Sabbath is about. I'm free. I don't *have* to do this, that, or the other thing. Christians do not even *have* to go to church. Obviously, Christians ought to want to go to church, and if they don't, some questions need to be asked. But in the sense that many parishioners come to church mainly out of a sense of obligation, they are not experiencing the Sabbath. Now I do hope they feel some sense of obligation, but if they are coming mainly out of obligation then they're not experiencing freedom. They're not experiencing the freedom to be before God to celebrate a relationship and a standing. This is the sense in which the Sabbath is a holiday: it is a time to rejoice in the fact that my worth is not in my ability to produce; it is a time to delight in the fact that my security does not rest in my ability to take care of myself; it is a time to reflect on the wonderful truth that God has set me free to be truly and simply me in the light of His love.

What have we learned about work thus far? We work because it is a part of the task God has given to us. If we are to bring the earth to its fullest potential, it will take our best efforts. On the other hand, work is not the key to our existence and cannot provide complete fulfillment. We were not made for work, but for God, and whenever we try to root our whole identity in work, we will miss something of what we were made for. This truth is underscored in the teachings on the Sabbath, where we are shown that rest is "superior" to work in the sense that rest is what work gives way to. Work is fundamental to human existence, but it is not ultimate. Whenever we try to make it so, it becomes an idol and can only bring frustration and bondage.

F I V E

WORK: WHAT IT IS AND WHAT IT ISN'T

When we consider the Bible's view of work, we see again the book's wonderful realism and sense of balance. On the one hand, laziness and idleness achieved through oppression are roundly denounced. Without any question, refusal to earn one's own livelihood is a sin. But if refusing to work is evil, this does not mean that working all the time is necessarily a virtue. The Bible makes it plain that work is a means, not an end.

Obviously, leisure was only available to those people in the biblical world who were rich. The Scriptures take a two-sided view of riches. On the one hand, riches are spoken of as a sign of blessing resulting from hard work, wisdom, and prudence. A couple of typical examples would be: "Diligent hands bring wealth" (Prov. 10:4, NIV) and "Humility and the fear of the Lord bring wealth and honor and life" (Prov. 22:4, NIV). But riches that are the result of shrewdness and crookedness and double-dealing are an offense to God. So, for instance, "Better a little with righteousness than much gain with injustice" (Prov. 16:8, NIV), and "He who increases his wealth by exorbitant interest amasses it for another, who will be kind to the poor" (Prov. 28:8, NIV). I have consciously taken all of these references from the Book of Proverbs because it is often suggested that this book always views the presence of wealth as a sign of divine blessing. Obviously that is not the case, and the same positions can be duplicated from a number of other books. The point is plain: whenever freedom from work rests on oppression and bondage it is evil.

AM I AN OPPRESSOR?

But when are my income and my leisure the result of oppression? Many of us today who are not in any way involved in direct oppression are made to carry a good deal of guilt over our supposed participation in oppression at second and third hand. The issues revolving around South Africa at the present time are a good case in point. I don't have any simple answers for that kind of question. All of us are going to have to bare our own souls before God, without trying to excuse ourselves, and come to a place where we can stand with good conscience. Without doubt, this kind of issue is a difficult one to sort out, but it is one each of us has to work with and wrestle with. We each have a share in the policies of our country, and if for example our wealth rests heavily on such a practice as buying raw materials from Third World countries at prices that lock those countries into poverty, then we must deal with that.

But I am more concerned about those matters that concern us directly. Is there any sense in which in some way I am using people to get some advantage for myself? If there is, then God have mercy on me and help me straighten that out. This is something that many of our Puritan forebears didn't hear very well. For instance, there is an Andrew

Carnegie who was himself a devout man and for whose benefactions we can be devoutly thankful. Yet he seemed to have no understanding of the extent to which his millions were coming from his paying workers next to nothing.

It's amazing how your position affects your point of view on an issue of this sort. I was raised on a farm and my politics and economics, as well as my religion, have always tended toward the right. But at one point after I graduated from college, I worked in a factory that was owned by a prominent Christian layman. This gentleman was not harsh or unkind, nor was the workplace particularly unpleasant. But he made quite a point of paying his workers no more than the minimum while he himself was reaping a great deal of money from the enterprise. I surprised myself with some of my emerging thoughts on economics! Yes, he was taking many of the risks from which we workers were protected, and he was providing the brains and expertise to run the company, something most of us lacked. But did those differences entitle him to an income 10 times greater than that of his workers? Was there not some way in which the profits could be shared more equitably? Without question we are doing better on these matters today than in Carnegie's day. But when we talk about the blessing of riches, we had better be sure what the real source of those riches is.

Some today would suggest that superfluity of any sort is bad, while others would say that the infallible result of obedience to God is wealth. I think both are incorrect. The truth is between those extremes. There normally is material blessing from God when one lives in line with His principles, but to assume that all wealth is a sign of divine blessing or that poverty is a sign of disobedience is dead wrong. It was Jesus who did not have a place to lay His head and had but one suit of clothes to His name. And by the same token, when many modern, wealthy religionists piously "give the credit" to God for their wealth, I often wonder what God's response is. Did God do it or did they? Riches are a blessing, but when they are achieved through taking advantage of other people, they are a sin.

In all of this I have no interest in provoking false guilt. It can become very easy for me to think that because I did not directly, personally, earn a particular thing, then I ought not to enjoy it. That is only a reverse kind of pride that demands that I must do everything for myself. What I am advocating is that we all take a careful look at our lifestyles, preferably assisted by Christian brothers and sisters who will keep us honest, to see whether our leisure is growing out of our taking advantage of people. When we have done that and made whatever adjustments that examination leads to, we will still recognize that little of what we have do we really deserve. But that is the point at which to receive with gratitude, disperse with magnanimity, and enjoy. Over against the guilt and the false pride, the Christian response is to say that in the light of what I *can* do, in the light of the responsibility I *can* take, I will receive what is given me, knowing that I do not deserve it, but receiving it from God's hands and attempting to profit from it and become the best sort of person I can in the light of what's been given me.

For instance, why were any of us born in the United States? We didn't stand in line and draw lots; it just happened that way in God's providence. Do you ever feel a little bit guilty about that when you see television stories about Ethiopia or some other stricken place? I do. But then I have to say, and I think it's the voice of God, "The issue is not 'Why?' but 'Now what?' Receive the gift from My hand and become all that you can in the light of receiving it." Then we will share not out of stingy guilt, but out of glad gratitude.

NO SPONGING!

A fifth specific scriptural principle regarding work is that refusal to work is a sin. Let me refer you to two passages: Proverbs 6:6-11 and 2 Thessalonians 3:6-12. They are too long to quote here so let me summarize them. In Proverbs we are told to look at the ant who works so steadily and are reminded that poverty awaits the person who lies around and sleeps all day. The 2 Thessalonians passage is Paul's famous one in which he says, "If a man will not work, he shall not eat." Not working is a sin. It's a sin for a person to sit around and sponge off other people when he could be providing for some of his own needs.

These passages and others make the Bible's, and God's, position quite clear. Each person is to accept responsibility for his own support. We are not to idly expect someone else to take care of us so that we can lounge around and do nothing. This says something of the divine view of human dignity. Since we can have a hand in supporting ourselves, we should. By the same token, to think that others should support me is to devalue them by making their needs subordinate to mine. God values each of us and invites each of us to cooperate with Him in meeting our needs.

Having said that, let me point out that the statement is a negative one. Not working is a sin. Shall we then immediately draw the conclusion that therefore work is virtuous? I don't think so. Both Paul and the writer of the Proverbs are speaking to people who had simply "checked out," people who refused to work. On the one hand is the lazy person, for whom work is too much trouble, and on the other is the religious enthusiast for whom work is much too mundane; it's much more fun to sit around discussing when Jesus will come back and take us out of this mess. The biblical writers are not telling these people how to find virtue, but how to avoid sin.

THE GOAL IS WISDOM

Well, if work in and of itself is not necessarily a virtue in Scripture, what is? Wisdom is. Wisdom is the highest virtue from the biblical point of view. What is wisdom? It is the ability to know what matters in life. It is the ability to look at life and weigh it and say, "These things endure and those things do not endure." Interestingly enough, this concept of wisdom is very close to the ideal Aristotle was talking about when he discussed the fruits of leisure.

So, yes, not working, refusing to work, refusing to take a hand in supplying my needs, that is bad. But I cannot then say, "Supplying my needs is the most important thing I can do in life." Although not working is a sin, the highest goal of life is not work, but wisdom. The person who has wisdom is able to take life in its wholeness and to unfold it and share it.

My children got a book from the library called *Frederick*, by Leo Lionni. At first I didn't like it very much. The more I thought about it, though, the more I liked it. The story goes like this: Some mice were collecting seeds during the summer. They were going at it like mad because winter was not far off. But one mouse, Frederick, just lay around. When the other mice got after him for being lazy, he said he was collecting for the winter too. So they left him alone and went about their business. They gathered all their little seeds, and winter came. Fortunately they didn't throw Frederick out as the ants did the grasshopper in Aesop's fable.

In the middle of the winter when everything was dark and gray and dismal and pointless, and they were nearing the end of their supply of seeds, Frederick said, "Now I'll bring out what I stored up." He had stored up the sound of the spring wind in the leaves. He had stored up the colors of the summer—the reds, the blues, the greens, the yellows. He had stored up the warmth of the sun. He had stored up words, words that flowed together like music and that seemed to make some sense out of life. By the time Frederick is through, it is clear that what he has stored up may be the most important of all. Yes, we must have food if we are to survive the winter, and that will take hard work to gather. But we must also have some things that make it worth living on through the winter until the next summer.

That story illustrates the truth that the person who gains wisdom has some important things to contribute to the society, things whose value is not apparent in terms of immediate usefulness. No, you can't eat the color of the sun filtering through the leaves. But on the other hand, if you can't look at the sun filtering through the leaves, maybe there's not much point in going on eating.

THE WISDOM OF THE PSALMS

We live not to work but to get a heart of wisdom. In the Bible this truth is perhaps best seen in the Psalms. There we see the discoveries of people who have experienced profound contemplation, people who have looked at the world, and at God, and at other people, people who have looked at life. The tone of the Psalms is so much different from that of so many contemporary songs. In these modern songs, life is always a disappointment. One singer said it all when she sang fifteen years ago, "Is that all there is?"

That's not the mode of the psalmists, is it? The psalmists have looked at life, and sometimes they have found things about life that they would rather not know. Yet these writers have not despaired. In Psalm 8 it says in effect, "When I think about the wonder of the universe, I just marvel at what You've done with humanity. It's so good of You." Psalm 19: "Those skies, that sun, they don't say a thing, but my, what they say! When I think about Your law; when I think about myself and my own tendency to kid myself; when I think about the possibility of being acceptable before You, I'm overwhelmed."

Then there is Psalm 139. Some years ago, I was sitting in a plane one day at the airport in Milwaukee with about 20 minutes before we went on somewhere and I thought, "Oh, what can I do with my time?" I *had* to use the time, you know! So I reached into my pocket and got my pocket Bible. But as I pulled it out I thought, "Now really, what would these Old Testament camel drivers say about a guy sitting here in an aluminum cigar tube about to shoot down a strip of concrete at a couple of hundred miles an hour and up into the air. They didn't know a thing about a life like that. What could they say to me?"

I don't remember whether I thought it or actually flipped open to it, but the words came, "If I take the wings of the morning, and dwell in the uttermost parts of the sea; even there shall Thy hand lead me" (vss. 9-10, KJV). That "camel driver" may not have known anything about Boeing; he may not have known anything about the speed of light; but he had looked long and carefully at the same world in which I live and had come to some profound understandings that are as relevant for Boeing as they were for camels.

How did the Psalms come to be? Yes, through the inspiration of the Holy Spirit. But, beyond that, there were people, thank God, who didn't have to spend all day grinding out the next meal. There were people who, like David, could take the time to think about and enjoy life. I'm so glad there were, because I need what David was able to derive from those leisure hours when he could think about what mattered and receive the truth that comes, not earned, but received.

ALL PLAY AND NO WORK?

None of this is to say that there is some sort of a hierarchy in life where the "Fredericks" among us are somehow better than the "mere gatherers." There is a balance that must be maintained. Both areas of life are necessary. I have to work *and* I need to make the time to think about what's important, whether I teach in a college or work in a steel mill. Certainly, when you take the mass of society you will find divisions of labor, but I don't think that dare be applied in a rigid way as in Plato's *Republic:* "Those are the philosopher kings, those are the drones." In the Christian idea of humanity there is an intermingling such as you see in the Apostle Paul. Paul said with a degree of pride, "I never took a cent from you folks. I gave you the Gospel for free and I worked in order to support myself." He goes on to say that, while this way is not obligatory, it was the way he chose to model an appropriate lifestyle for the Christian (2 Thes. 3:7-9). What Paul's example shows us is that, as Christians who know something of grace and possibility, we do not need to dichotomize our lives; we can bring together both the world of work and the world of contemplation and reflection.

Before we leave the Psalms, we must notice one other thing. Some of the more recent versions make plain through their footnotes what was not plain in the older versions. That is, that a number of the psalms are acrostics: each verse begins with a succeeding letter of the alphabet. Verse 1 begins with A, verse two begins with B, and so on. The most famous example is Psalm 119, where the paragraphs are acrostic. Why would someone take the time to do that? For the fun of it. Just because. What's the value of it? None, except to say that in some way in the beauty of the world, everything fits together. Alphabets have order; thought has order. Isn't it fun to see the two things and put them together? The psalmists didn't do that for usefulness, they did it for fun, for free; to express something about their feelings for the universe and the joy of putting things together.

This joy of putting things together is one of the reasons we enjoy puns: they put together things that appear to go together but really don't, and the incongruity is funny. Someone has said that puns are the lowest form of humor, but the Arabs and the Hebrews didn't think that. For them, the pun was the highest form of humor, because you were finding things that fit together in funny ways, and that says something about the way the world fits together in often funny ways.

What we have learned in this chapter is that work is not the ultimate virtue. Yes, it is important that each of us accept responsibility for our own support. Leisure that is the result of mere laziness or of oppression of the helpless is an offense to God. But diligence and industry are not the chief virtues to which God calls us. Rather, the chief virtue is wisdom, that insight into the nature and meaning of life that can only come to those who are able to lift their eyes and hearts from the grindstone of labor long enough to contemplate where they are and what is happening around them.

S I X

MOTIVATIONS FOR WORKING

Why do we work? What values does work have for us? Obviously, one of the values is subsistence. But aside from that what does work do for us? Two things come immediately to mind. One is worth, and the other is possessions. The person who works demonstrates a usefulness to his or her society, and that usefulness is an indication of worth. Work also supplies the means for the satisfaction of what seems to be a basic human drive—acquisitiveness. How does the Bible view these motivations? Are these adequate justifications for working?

WHY ARE WE IMPORTANT?

The issue of self-worth is a major one in our society today. It has been brought into sharper focus through the women's movement. For whatever reason, it has become a widespread sentiment that homemaking and child rearing are not "real" work. Perhaps this is because no salary is paid for this work. Somehow unless someone is willing to pay money for a behavior, that behavior is regarded as of no significance. At any rate, more and more women are working outside the home, not merely to add to the family income or to have some money of their own, but in many cases to demonstrate to themselves and their society that they are people óf worth.

Now we may deplore the view in which homemaking and child rearing are seen as menial, second-class occupations when in fact they are so vital to the existence of a healthy society. However, even if these tasks are restored to their rightful place of honor, that would not address our real question here: must a person do useful work in order to be of worth? If we succeed in demonstrating that homemaking is incredibly useful, much more so than disc-jockeying, for instance, is that the solution to the problem of worth? I don't think so, for if I understand the Bible correctly it says that worth is not determined by apparent utility.

This was brought home to me some years ago when I was reading James Michener's novel *Centennial.* In telling the story of the area in northeastern Colorado where the town of Centennial was to grow up, Michener devotes one chapter to an account of the Arapahoe Indians who lived in that region. The chapter revolves around the life of a particular brave, following him from childhood to death.

As I read the author's re-creation of the Arapahoe life, I became more and more uncomfortable. Although I was aware that Michener is no friend of Christianity and could be expected to demonstrate the superiority of other cultures wherever possible, I still had the feeling that even if he was exaggerating somewhat, the Arapahoe had a lot of qualities that were as good as, or in some cases even superior to, those of Christians.

Then I reached the end of the chapter. There the central figure decides to sacrifice himself in order to obtain horses for the tribe. The neighboring Pawnee had horses, but the Arapahoe did not, and the Pawnee took every advantage of that situation. So the brave, now an old man, had himself tied to a stake within shouting distance of the Pawnee village. There he began to shout curses and taunts at the Pawnee, daring them to come out and get him. Finally they could stand it no longer and rushed out to kill him. But while they were doing that, the Arapahoe men slipped into the corral on the other side of the village and stole all the horses.

Now to the point of this story. When word of the brave's death reached the Arapahoe village, the rest of the women went in and stripped his wife of everything she owned, including her tepee, and left her to die. In their defense, Michener points out that a widow filled no useful function in the tribe and that the tribe could not afford to feed a noncontributing mouth.

GOD'S CRITERION FOR WORTH

When I read this incident I thought, *Aha, there's the difference!* for the Bible makes it crystal clear that utility is not the criterion of value. Who are the people who are under God's special care? The widow, the orphan, and the stranger (Ex. 22:21-24; Deut. 10:18-19; Ps. 68:5; Isa. 1:17). These people were no more useful to the Israelites than they were to the Arapahoe. But God says that these people are under His special protection. Why would He do that? Because value is not a function of utility. These people are of value because they *are.* I'm glad to be a Christian, to be a product of the Bible, every time I run into that. People are of value just because they are.

Now what does that mean for our consideration here? It means that work can become a trap. If my worth depends on my ability to do useful, that is, in our society, remunerative, work, what happens when I can't do that, whether because of illness or unemployment or age? It means I am worthless. What does the Bible say to that? No! Your worth does not depend on your utility as determined by work.

How can the Bible make a statement like that? Human worth is in our bearing of the divine image, not in anything else. We are ends, not means to some other end. We do not exist *for* something else in creation; in fact, we do not even exist *for* God in a real sense. To be sure, we exist only because of Him, but He does not want to use us for something, only to enjoy us and be enjoyed by us. Thus it is precisely those who are least useful in human terms who are marked out as God's special favorites. They prove that it can never be thought that utility is the source of value.

But why is it that we are always falling into the "utility equals worth" trap? Surely it is because of our deeply ingrained need to take care of ourselves and to be independent. The whole idea that my identity might be found in my relationship to someone else is repugnant to me. This means that it is only the person who "carries his own weight," who "pulls his own load," who can hold his head up in society. "I don't need to depend on anybody; I take care of myself." We dread being a "burden" to someone else. Thus it is very difficult for us to entrust the supply of our needs to someone else. This perhaps explains why paid work is so important. It is not even enough to believe that we are making a contribution to our society. It must be a contribution that rewards us by giving us the means to feel that we need depend on no one else.

But as I said above, this view is a trap. It does not give us a sense of self-worth independent of circumstances. Instead, we only have that sense when we are working. When we are not working, we are deprived of worth. Work all too

73

easily becomes an end in itself. If my worth and independence are the result of work, then work quickly comes to fill my whole horizon, demanding a place in my life that cannot be filled by anything else very easily.

Thus, the Bible tells us that though work is a good thing, it is not the source of our worth before God. In fact, if we try to make it the source of our worth, it is very likely to undermine that worth, because we will only have it when working for pay. In this sense work can very easily become an idol, a replacement for the true God, through which we try to satisfy our own needs.

WORKING TO OWN THINGS

Another specific principle that speaks to the biblical concept of work is found in the parable of the rich man and his barns (Luke 12:13-21). He thought that when he had enough things to keep him in comfort for the rest of his life, he had nothing more to worry about. He also thought that securing his physical well-being was of prime importance in his life. In fact, as Jesus says at the beginning of the story, "A man's life does not consist of the abundance of his possessions" (Luke 12:15). Most of us have a very hard time believing that. Probably we would phrase it another way entirely, such as, "The real quality of a person's life is directly proportional to the number of his or her possessions." But however we feel about it, Jesus is saying that the true goal of life is something other than possessions.

Just before the statement of Jesus quoted above, He tells His listeners to beware of all covetousness. Yes, when everything is said and done, our desire to possess and own is nothing more nor less than covetousness. That takes us back to the tenth commandment. Have you ever thought about the significance of the placement of that command-

ment? Why is it the last? And what is its relat
first? (By the way, thinking this way, makin
connections, is one of the fruits of leisure we
earlier. But back to the main point!)

The first commandment requires us to acknowledge no
other gods. Most of us in the United States feel fairly smug
about that. We have no idols and don't expect to have any.
But how about the tenth commandment? The Ten Commandments are divided into two groups: the first four concern how we relate to God and the last six concern how we
relate to other people. But while the command against
coveting is clearly one of those that concern our relationship with others, it stands a bit apart from the others. The
fifth through ninth deal primarily with actions: honoring
parents, not killing, not committing adultery, not stealing,
and not lying. Unlike these the tenth does not speak primarily of an action, but of an attitude, and of a very generalized
one. What is going on here?

GREED AND IDOLATRY

I think this tenth command is saying much the same thing
as the first, but from a different angle. At the beginning and
the end of the list of commands the same issue is dealt
with—we must not have any other gods in our lives than the
Lord. Acquisitiveness—covetousness—is a denial of the
true God. That may seem a bit strange at first. But on two
occasions we are told that covetousness is idolatry (Eph.
5:5; Col. 3:5), and in two other references the two concepts
are put together in such a way as to make the connection
clear (Isa. 57:17; 1 Cor. 5:11).

What does that mean? Yes, greed, or acquisitiveness, is
bad, even evil, but how can it be equated with idolatry? First
of all, we must put out of our heads the idea that idolatry,

which is the worship of other gods, necessarily involves the use of little statues. The little statues are only a means of making visible where one's true commitment lies. But it is not necessary to have the statues in order to have the commitment. Where is the commitment of the idolater? It is to the supplying of needs through this world; it is to the belief, practically speaking, that this physical world is all there is and that our real needs can be met through the manipulation of that world. This is idolatry, and our covetousness is an expression of that commitment.

At the present time most of us do not invoke the spirits of this world to help us achieve our covetous goals, but that is only because of our naturalistic and mechanistic views of the world. Our pagan forebears, who had a little more experience with this than we do, recognized that there are spirits animating the physical world and that those spirits must be taken account of. We, who have had the antispiritual views of the last century ingrained into our minds, are only slowly coming to see the fallacies of that position and to recognize the spiritual dimension. The rapidly increasing interest in astrology and the occult in recent years bears testimony to that growing recognition.

But someone says, "I still don't see how to desire things is to deny God and become an idolater." Let me put it this way. Something in us says that if we just had all the things we can imagine, we would be happy. Is that true? No, it is damnably false. That suggests that the deepest longings of the human heart can be satisfied by this created world. That is not so.

WHAT MAKES US HAPPY?
Jesus says in that part of the Sermon on the Mount that we call the Beatitudes that the only truly happy person is the

one who has learned how to own nothing, to deny the bodily appetites, to bear the burdens of the world, and to forget about appearances (Luke 6:20-26). Those are much more radical words than most of us care to read. What is He saying? He is saying that our only source of happiness—eternal happiness—is in our relationship to God, the God who made this world and loves it, but is not part of it. The idea that you and I can produce our own happiness by acquiring a superfluity of this world's goods through our own efforts at manipulating this world results in infinite, eternal loss. So the tenth commandment says to us to be careful. We may congratulate ourselves on having kept all the other commandments remarkably well when in fact, because of our covetousness, we haven't even gotten by the first.

But someone says, "Fine, so covetousness is a bad thing, even worse than I had imagined. What does that have to do with work and leisure?" Just this: why do you and I work? What is the real motive? Isn't it all too often so that we can live in the style to which we would *like* to become accustomed? Don't we work in too many cases merely to satisfy our covetousness? When that is true, what does it mean? It means that our work has become forced labor in the shrine of the gods of this world. When that has happened work is not a good thing but an evil. Now we work not because we wish to, but because we must. And because the thirst for things, like all thirsts for anything less than the Creator, is insatiable, we must work more and more for less and less.

So again, as with the preceding principle, the Bible says that work is good, but that when work is solely or largely an attempt to satisfy covetous desires, it is prostituted in the service of a false god. Our God calls us to a freedom in which our work is not compelled or driven; it is free.

THE BIBLE'S VIEW OF WORK

We have now completed our look at the eight biblical statements relating to work and leisure. Before we move on, let me summarize what the Bible has said. Without question work, biblically speaking, is significant and important. We are expected to be involved in productive labor. The Bible does not say that the elite—the leisure class—are the important people and that those who have to work are merely the drones who may be ignored. It says it is important that people be involved in the production of their livelihood. But it does not say that the production of their livelihood is the source of their meaning and existence.

Much of what the Bible is saying about what work is and isn't can be expressed in the contrast between "being" and "doing." Work is something all of us are called to do and in which we are expected to find a measure of fulfillment. The problem arises when we see work not merely as something to do, but as the source of our being. It is at this point that the curse begins to take effect. For our being is not in our hands to create or alter. We would like to have it in our hands, just as Adam and Eve wanted it there. We would like to be able to determine who we are by our own efforts. But that is not what work was designed for, and to attempt to use work for something for which it was not designed is to deliver ourselves into its hands as its slave.

This is the nature of the curse. Work itself is not the curse any more than are childbearing and family relations. Rather, God has made the world so that any attempt to find ultimate significance in anything other than Him is to find ourselves frustrated and, if we persist in trying to use creation in those wrong ways, enslaved. One need only think of drugs or alcohol or sex as examples of what I am saying. When work is used as an expression of the being we already have because of the work of God within us, then it is an avenue of blessing. But the being comes from God, not from work.

Some early preachers of holiness, which is my heritage, preached the possibility of complete restoration from the Fall. According to that interpretation the Christian who has experienced the fullness of the Spirit should no longer find his or her work frustrating. If that's true, I fear I have not received the gift of the Spirit, because I often find my work very frustrating. I often find it unfulfilling. At the same time I have to say that there are many, many days when I say, "Lord, I shouldn't be getting paid for this. I like it too much." What I am saying is that we will, until we are glorified, continue to experience some of the effects of the fall of the race. While many of us will find a large measure of fulfillment in our work, we will never find it wholly satisfying lest we try to use it to fill the void in our lives that only God can fill.

PART THREE
GOD'S VIEW OF LEISURE

S E V E N

CREATION

So far in our study we have looked at three basic questions and eight specific scriptural statements relating to work and leisure. Let's take the next step in exploring God's view of leisure, which is to look for general concepts that shed light on the topic.

The first of these basic concepts is creation. What does the doctrine of creation say to us about the nature and meaning of leisure? First of all, this doctrine is perhaps *the* fundamental doctrine of the Bible. From this truth stem all the rest. Creation is the fundamental expression of the character of the biblical God. Whatever else He is, He is first and foremost the Creator. That's where we begin in the Scripture, and that's the theme that occurs again and again and again throughout the Book.

WHAT IS CREATION?
What is so significant about this concept? First we need to be sure just what we are talking about. What is the idea of

creation? It is the idea that all things that exist sprang from the mind and will of a single divine Being. The Hebrew word is *bara'*, and it suggests the making of something brand new, something that never existed before. Now, what is so significant about that?

First of all, this idea of creation is unique to the Bible. In the other ancient stories of the beginning of the world, there is no creation as such. All things proceed out of preexisting stuff, often by accident or afterthought, or as a by-product of a cosmic struggle between the gods, who themselves came out of that primordial matter. If you take the personal and spiritual elements out of these stories, they sound very much like modern "scientific" theories about the origin of things. When you think about it, that's not too surprising. If ancient brilliant people and modern brilliant people both try to explain this world by starting with this world as their only data, it is not strange if they come out with the same general explanation.

But the Hebrews, who make no claims to be particularly brilliant either scientifically or spiritually, come out at a radically different point. They tell us that it is spirit and mind that have always existed and that the material cosmos does not exist by chance or as a by-product, but because of the specific intention of that Spirit, whose motivation and essence are love. Personally, I find no satisfactory explanation for why the Hebrews alone should have come up with this revolutionary idea other than the explanation they give—God told them!

Purpose. What are some of the implications of this amazing idea? First and foremost is purpose. Everything that exists has a purpose. Nothing exists by chance, but rather everything that is has come out of the mind of the sovereign Creator. That means everything is significant. The Milky Way is significant, but so is an amoeba. It means that human experience is worth studying and evaluating and that we can determine what is right and wrong according to the Creator's purpose. It means that we can decide whether progress is being made toward the fulfillment of that purpose. Deny creation and you must deny purpose. Deny purpose and you must deny right and wrong. Deny right and wrong and you must cease to evaluate. Here lies the sticking point in modern culture, for we blithely deny creation, purpose, and moral law, but we still want to evaluate. But on what basis and to what end? We are like Israel in the time of the Judges: "In those days there was no king in Israel; every man did that which was right in his own eyes" (Jud. 21:25, KJV).

Design. The second thing the doctrine of creation teaches us is that the order or design we see in the universe is not a result of chance or natural selection. Rather it is the result of the operation of a loving divine mind, who both conceived of creation and brought it into being. Without creation there really is no explanation for the order we find in our world, and in fact we must believe, as do many modern artists and philosophers, that the whole idea of order and harmony is merely an illusion. When this belief is carried to its logical extreme, as it is in many quarters today, there is no reason to study our world, to reflect lovingly upon it, because whatever might be discovered in such study would be illusory anyway. I am personally convinced that the decline of interest in science today is not accidental. For the secular humanist there is no real order, no real unity, no real purpose in the world, so why study it? This is exactly why the great ancient cultures of the Nile Valley and of Mesopotamia produced no real science. It is not because they were stupid, as complacent 19th- and 20th-century parochialism would like to believe. No, it is because their view of the world would not let them do so. The pre-

Christian Greeks came to a view of the order and harmony of the universe on the basis of pure logic, but lacking the religious underpinning to support such a view, they soon lost it. It was only when Greek logic found a basis in the Christian worldview that genuine science began to be practiced in the West. Today, as the late Francis Schaeffer pointed out, the engine of science runs on the terrific momentum built up previously, but the concept of creation that fueled that engine has all too widely disappeared, leaving the engine to slowly run down.

Meaning. If there is purpose and design in creation, then there is meaning. Everything that happens, everything that *is,* is important. Our lives, our work, our hopes, and our dreams are not insignificant. Somehow they fit in with a grand master strategy for all things, and nothing is lost. I love the *King James Version*'s rendering of the eighth verse of Psalm 56, "Thou tellest my wanderings; put Thou my tears into Thy bottle: are they not in Thy book?"

This idea of meaning does not require that we think of God as having some master blueprint that He drew up before time began and into which He continually forces us. Rather His creativity makes it possible for Him to take the results of our choices, good and bad, and weave those results into the accomplishment of His overall purposes. The picture here is not of an architect but of a military strategist, who is able to see how to make the vicissitudes of the individual battles work together to accomplish his overall goal.

Freedom. The fourth thing the doctrine of creation teaches us is freedom. This Creator, this One who has envisioned a cosmos and then brought it into existence—He has not done it out of obligation. In fact, He would have been better off from one point of view if He hadn't created this mess. He wouldn't have had to endure the crucifixion of His Son. He wouldn't have had to endure sin. And certainly, in His infinite wisdom and knowledge, He recognized all of that. Yet He chose to do it.

Why did He choose to do it? In the terms of Proverbs 8, He did it for the sheer joy of it. In this lovely passage of Scripture, Wisdom is speaking about her function in the creation. She says,

When He established the heavens, I was there,
when He drew a circle on the face of the deep,
   when He made firm the skies above,
   when He established the fountains of the deep,
   when He assigned to the sea its limit, so that
     the waters might not transgress His command,
   when He marked out the foundations of the earth,
   then I was beside Him, like a master workman;
and I was daily His delight, rejoicing before Him
  always,
rejoicing in His inhabited world and delighting in
  the sons of men. (Proverbs 8:27-31, RSV)

Why did He create? He created for the pure joy of it. Why does an artist paint? Why does a composer compose? Why does a preacher preach? For joy! There is a compulsion there, but it is the compulsion of joy.

It has always seemed to me that one of the indications of God's joy in creation is its abundance. Haven't you wondered why there are hundreds of kinds of the same thing? Surely four or five kinds of flowers would have been enough. But no, there are tulips and irises and lilies and roses and sweet williams and may apples and more into the thousands and perhaps tens of thousands. The same thing is true with the animals. Surely whoever did that did it for the fun of it and not because it was useful. Take trees for example: if you only needed trees for lumber, a couple of hardwoods and a couple of softwoods would have served.

But no, there are maples and birches and oaks and larches and tamaracks and many, many more. Creativity means freedom and in that freedom there is joy.

FROM POSSIBILITY TO REALITY

What then is creativity? For one thing, it is the capacity to conceive of, to imagine, to picture. The second part of it is of course the capacity to bring that vision to fruition. God is the Creator with the capacity to envision something that doesn't exist and also to bring that thing into existence.

Dr. Robert A. Traina, professor of English Bible at Asbury Theological Seminary, illustrates these characteristics of creativity in his lectures on the Book of Genesis. He calls attention to the recurring refrain in chapter 1 of Genesis: "It was good.... It was good.... It was very good," and asks what is the meaning and significance of that refrain. Surely God does not mean to say that the material world is morally good, for trees and rocks and worms and seas are morally neutral. Dr. Traina suggests, and I think he is correct, that they are the words of an artist, an artist who has seen a picture in his mind and has now transferred that picture onto canvas. He steps back to view the finished product critically and says, "Uh-huh, that's it; it's good." What is He saying? He is saying what no human artist can fully say: "Yes, that is just what I envisioned; it's perfect."

"But," you say, "what does all this have to do with leisure?" Much indeed. As I mentioned in an earlier chapter, it seems to me that this capacity to create, the capacity to dream of possibilities that are not, is one of the areas in which the image of God appears in us. How is it that we can think of something that does not yet exist? We almost routinely imagine what has never been in all the history of the universe and set about to bring it to pass. Where does that ability come from? It comes from our sharing the image of our Creator. And *that* means that we are most fully human, most fully experiencing our uniqueness, when we are being most creative.

I'M NO ARTIST!

But someone says, "Now wait a minute, I'm not creative at all. I have trouble getting a paint-by-number picture to look right! Are you telling me that I have to become an artist or a sculptor or a gourmet cook to be fully human?" You can relax, I'm not saying that at all. What I am saying is that we all have our own potentials for planning something, for dreaming, and for bringing it to fruition, and that leisure time is not wasted time when it gives us the opportunity to experience those potentials. In fact, that is the time when we are freed to become like God. If our work time leaves us feeling driven, compelled, shut in to the constraints of "how it must be done," as much work does, then time to become re-humanized is imperative, and there is nothing more re-humanizing than creative activity.

But still the question is, "What can I do?" Frequently there is a lot of baggage in the form of inferiority feelings, perfectionism, and whatnot that comes along with that question. But *what* we do is much less important than that we do something. It is the Enemy of our souls who tells us that nothing we can ever do measures up and that we would be much better off just doing nothing and subsiding into a mass of self-consumed feelings. I remember a cartoon my wife, Karen, kept on our family bulletin board, the refrigerator, for a long time. A disheveled little girl is standing in the doorway of the kitchen with a blackened cookie sheet in her hands. On the sheet is a single black circle. The mother, with horror on her face, is looking at the little girl and past her into the kitchen, which looks very much as though a bomb had gone off in it. But on the little girl's face is a beatific smile of accomplishment, satisfaction, and excitement as she holds up her blackened cookie sheet and says, "I baked a cookie!" Yes! When in the freedom of our own minds we dream of something, however small and insignificant by some standards, when we plan how to do it and do it, however imperfectly by anyone else's standards, in that experience we are sharing the life and being of our Creator.

GOOD-FOR-NOTHING VALUE

If the creative possibilities in each of us are to be realized, we must not only overcome our perfectionism, we must also learn that a thing is the more valuable when it is not good for anything. On the face of it that is a rather shocking statement. It appears to say that something is valuable when it is valueless, an obvious contradiction in terms. But that's not what I am saying. What I am saying is that the value of a thing or a thought must be determined apart from its utility. In fact, when we value something *because* it is useful—good for something—we devalue the thing itself. In other words, if a certain object is good for something, it's the something that has value and the object can be thrown away when the something has been gotten. But if the object is not good for something else, then it has the potential of being good in itself, of being valuable for itself.

Now what does that have to do with our creativity? Just this: if I am often unwilling to indulge my creative urges because what I do will not be perfect, I am also often unwilling because the things I make or think about won't be good for anything. But creativity does not need to consider that. God did not create for utility; He created for joy.

I thought of that again the other day as I was driving

along a wintry road. It has been a very dry winter here and things look unusually drab. But there on the roadside were three male cardinals, heart-stabbingly red against their dull surroundings. Oh, I know all the reasons some wooden heart could give as to why a cardinal is just that shade of red, but I don't believe them. *That* shade of red is an expression of our God's pure joy in creating, and utility has very little to do with it. So, like Him, we need to create for joy and not for utility. Of course, when we create something that is useful, that is fine. I do not mean to devalue utility. It is certainly of value to create something useful, but when we create something for itself alone, that is when we create something truly valuable.

Most inventions, I am told, were not created in order to solve some known problem but simply as a result of creative experimentation—creative play, if you will. Then the problem was to find something to do with what had been discovered. Creation of the thing itself came first; utility was secondary. A recent newspaper article told of the invention of that product that is such a godsend to all poor cooks like me—Teflon. A researcher was experimenting with refrigeration gases, storing them in containers packed in dry ice. One of the containers registered no pressure and seemed to be empty. However, when the researcher weighed it, it weighed as much as the others. Opening it, he found it full of a slippery, powdery substance. Eureka, Teflon! Having discovered it, there were wonderful things to do with it. But the discovery was a result of pure creativity.

FREEDOM'S LIMITS
Let me make one final comment about the implications of the doctrine of creation. Although our creativity involves

freedom, that freedom has constraints. For no one of us is the Creator. We follow in the footsteps of the Creator; we are creatures. One of our problems today is our insistence on absolute freedom without regard for the structure of the created world. Without going off into wild flights of fancy, it seems to me that what is beautiful, what is good, what is true has to be in touch with the structure of creation, and what falls outside those boundaries is not simply "good for nothing" but useless and valueless. A thing that denies the character of creation, a thing that is formless and lacking in harmony, does not bring us nearer to life; rather it alienates us from life.

By the same token that which is trivial but masquerades as high art alienates us from reality as well. It is one thing for you and me to do something of a minor nature, such as a paint-by-number picture, and feel a sense of accomplishment and release in it. But it is quite different for an "artist" to paint a monstrous picture of a soup can and call that creativity. That may be a statement about reality, all right, but it is a statement in stark contradiction to what the Bible tells us about reality.

Whenever we create something, we are becoming more human. Some people have greater creative abilities than others. But all of us, whoever we are, can participate in this aspect of the image of God in some way. It may be gardening, or woodworking, or cooking, or painting, or writing, or a handicraft, or a hundred other things, but whenever we take the opportunity to plan something and bring it to a fruition that will be satisfying, we're maximizing what makes us different from the animals. This is the possibility that our new bonanza of leisure holds out to us, the opportunity to experience our true humanity through the medium of creativity.

E I G H T

GRACE

We move now to a second scriptural principle that has a bearing on a Christian view of leisure, the principle of grace. If the doctrine of creation is the foundation stone of biblical theology, then the doctrine of grace is the capstone. For in this doctrine is all that is unique to the biblical concept of the relationship between God and human beings. Each of the great religions can be summed up with a key word: for Islam it is *submission;* for Buddhism it is *denial;* for Hinduism it is *unity;* for Confucianism it is *wisdom.* What is it for biblical religion, and for Christianity in particular? Surely it is the word *grace.*

Grace, the idea that human beings can never earn their way through righteous living or manipulate their way through correct performance of religious ritual into the eternal presence of God. Grace, the idea that God Himself has done everything for us that needs to be done to ensure a right relationship between us and Himself and offers us eternal life in His presence for free. How incredible and unique! All the rest of the world religions emphasize struggle and effort, performance and achievement. Over against them is a religion that does not speak of our toiling up toward God, but of God graciously stepping across the barriers of infinity to come to us, gifts overflowing from His hands. Yes, Christianity is certainly unique, unique in its explanation of the origins of all things, but it is also unique in its resolution of the problem of human-divine relationships.

The concept of grace is a fascinating one. Have you ever thought about it? What do we mean when we talk about the "grace of God"? Those of us who have been raised in the church probably have a fairly good idea, but think about the problem of the person who comes in off the street in deciphering what in the world we are talking about. The church usage is so much different from the everyday usage. For instance, what do we mean when we talk about a person's having grace? We are saying something about bearing and style and appropriateness of action. But that's not what we mean when we talk about God's grace, is it? What *is* the Bible saying? Think about such a statement as "Noah found grace in the eyes of the Lord" (Gen. 6:8, KJV). When God looked at Noah, He saw good things in Noah. Did Noah deserve that, had he earned it? Not really. No, God's grace is His ability to look at us and see grace in us, even when our lives may seem to us just one clumsy blunder after another. A fascinating thing happens when someone sees good things in us. We begin to act more nearly in the way that person sees us. Think of an oafish young fellow who is loved by a charming young woman. You and I may say, "I don't know what she sees in him," but see she does, and how often her seeing what none of the rest of us could or cared to see brings those very qualities out in him. This is part of the way God's grace, His ability to see grace in us, operates.

THE PROBLEM OF PRIDE

But it is very difficult for us to accept God's grace. Why is that? It is because of the fundamental problem of the human race—pride. In an earlier chapter I talked about the deep-seated nature of the problem of covetousness, growing out of our need to care for ourselves. But underneath our covetousness is the sin of pride. This is the most damnable sin in the biblical catalog. It is the root of all our other sins, including greed, sexual impurity, gossip, and self-righteousness. Pride is that voice within, whether whining or triumphant, that says, "I can make it without God." This is the source of all our idolatry, our self-preoccupation. This is the source of our need for self-justification. We must prove to the world (but perhaps most of all to ourselves) that we deserve to exist, that we deserve to be taken seriously, that we deserve certain rights and privileges. It is pride that says, "I only want what I have earned. I only want what I can say I have produced." In this way, my work becomes my means of self-justification. "I have produced this; therefore, I am somebody. I have earned this; therefore, I am somebody."

A manifestation of this problem in us is our difficulty in receiving gifts. Now of course it's not so hard if we can tell ourselves that we deserve this special treatment because of our exalted position or our selfless work or whatever. That is pride manifesting itself in another way. But suppose we can't really make ourselves believe that any of those good reasons are true. How do we feel when we receive a gift that just flat out is not deserved? It's kin isn't it? Now that's an interesting word to ating? Why humbling? Because our warp though we should not have anything we ha earned. That gift is a reflection on our abil ourselves, to pay our own way.

So what happens when we have received that gift we don't deserve or when we have been invited out to dinner by someone who didn't have to? We start planning how to pay them back! Our pride cannot stand to think that we are in someone's debt. "I can pay my own way! I can take care of myself."

EARNING OUR WAY

Because pride is so deeply ingrained in us, it is hard for us to see what it really means. But pride is the reason there will be "good" people in hell. Now wait just a minute! If a person has really done his or her best, has tried to do what's right, do you mean to tell me God's going to send them to hell? No, actually, as C.S. Lewis illustrates so beautifully in his book *The Great Divorce*, God will *let* such persons go to hell. If we have really served our own pride all of our lives, as those who attempt to justify themselves by their own righteousness have, heaven will be a most terrifying place.

But pride taints all my efforts to live a good life. What are we saying, all of us good church folks, when we insist on going to heaven on account of our good lives? We're saying, "I can get there on my own. I can be good enough so that God will one day have to say, 'My, my, I didn't think you could, but you've done it. You've earned your way into heaven. Congratulations!' " Pride says, "If I can't earn my way to heaven, I'm not sure I want to go there."

This is the reason for Jesus' harsh words to the religious people of His day, when He said to them that many whom they wouldn't expect would enter heaven before they would (Luke 13:22-30). He was not suggesting that unrepentant sinners could enjoy God's grace but that those people who ow they are sinners and who know they can never make their own are far closer to heaven than those who in their pride feel sure they can earn their way in.

How easily we forget that all we really earn by our proud attempts to take care of ourselves is death! We earn not only physical death, but also what John calls the second death—separation from God forever (Rev. 2:11). Paul is quite clear on the issue: "The wages of sin is death" (Rom. 6:23, KJV). And pride is *the* sin.

But maybe we need to talk about that a bit more, for pride is a fairly positive idea in our thinking. After all, people have to take a little pride in their work, don't they? And a little pride in oneself, a little self-respect, is a good thing, isn't it? Isn't a low sense of self-esteem really bad?

What about this? Why is pride so bad? How can I say that it is the root of all sin? Pride is evil because it is in direct contradiction to the foundation of our existence. We were made to be dependent creatures, dependent on God for our very lives. But pride says, "I will be dependent on no one. I will determine what is right and wrong for me (Gen. 3:1-7) and I will do what I want when I want." There is no clearer picture of this than in Isaiah 14, a passage often said to describe Satan and his pride. However modestly it is cloaked, pride says, "I will be God." But death mocks all such foolish pretensions. How can you and I, mortal to the core, have such monumental presumption as to think that *we* could be God for ourselves?

So the Apostle Paul is absolutely right. What have we earned with our prideful efforts? What is in our pay envelopes at the end of the day? Death. But grace says, "You don't have to take your pay envelope, thank God." Now that sounds almost sacrilegious. "What, not take my pay envelope, and be thankful for not having to take it?" It is very hard for us to believe that anything unearned could possibly be good, yet grace says, "It's free. Come and get it."

NO FREE LUNCH?

It's interesting to watch the faces in a congregation, a staid, socially acceptable congregation, when you preach on grace. You see the shades going down behind their eyes, and you know what they are thinking: "There are no free lunches." "You only get what you pay for, buddy." "You're talking about everybody going on welfare, aren't you?" "You're talking about nobody working." Something deep within us revolts against the idea of grace.

This grace that runs through Christianity is free; there is nothing you or I can do to earn it. All we can do is take it. Now that's fun. That's the delight of the child. Tell a child something is free and she doesn't ask, "Did I deserve it?" "Did I earn it?" She's in the middle of it! But the adult says, "I mustn't enjoy it; it's not mine. I didn't earn it." Pride becomes an imperative driving us through our lives saying, "You've got to prove your worth, buddy, sister! Prove it! Prove it!" Prove it? To whom?

In this contemporary age people think there must be a catch to anything that's free. There must be an angle to it. And so we look at Jesus on the cross and say, "What's His angle? Why should He do that? It's not logical." To us, only self-serving is logical. Yet, grace delights in incongruity. It delights in things that don't fit conventional wisdom. According to conventional wisdom only the elder son has the right to carry the family name, but grace confers that right on the younger. In that same light, it was John the Baptist who was here first, but it's the One who comes after him who receives the honor.

GRACE'S SENSE OF HUMOR

Grace laughs at the incongruities of life, the strange turnings, the funny things. Pride cannot do that; everything is too serious. Everything must be watched carefully to be sure that we are not being shortchanged. But God in His grace has the power to conquer whatever may happen with joy. So He laughs at the seriousness with which this world's rulers plot to storm heaven. Psalm 2 tells the story: "He who sits in the heaven will have them in derision." God looks at a world in revolt and laughs! He says, "Ha, ha! That's the funniest thing I've ever seen. Look at that! Ha, ha." We more often picture a stern, worried God whose position is threatened saying, "Oh, what am I going to do now? Oh my, they're destroying My plans again. I can't let this happen. Oh, dear." We don't envision the infinitely capable, infinitely creative One who laughs at our infantile rantings, knowing that His grace is stronger than our wildest rebellions.

Think of another of grace's jokes. Look at a shaggy-bearded old man and a wizened old woman. What is that in their arms? It's a brand-new, spanking fresh baby! And what have they named him? They have named him "God laughed." Why? Because God says, "That's the funniest thing I've ever seen. Look at those two!" And you hear the ring of laughter all through the story. Earlier, when God was visiting with Abraham, He had said, "Abraham, when I come back here next year you and Sarah are going to have a baby." And this pious, saintly old man falls down on the ground laughing. He says, "God, that's the funniest thing I ever heard. Tell me another one." Now before you accuse me of irreverence with the sacred text, go look at it. There it is. Grace can laugh, and those who know the grace of God can laugh. They can even laugh at the incongruity of grace's promises. That's all right. You remember that Sarah laughed too. My wife, Karen, told me that if anybody told her she was going to have a baby when she was 99 she'd laugh too, but it would probably be hysteria. The incongruities! That's grace!

Think of another of grace's jokes. How will God save the world? Through a peasant baby in a barn, that's how. Now that's not the way I would have done it. Salvation is much too serious a matter to mess around with babies and barns. But not for grace. Grace is free.

THE FLESH AND THE SPIRIT

That's ultimately what "the flesh" and "the spirit" are about in the Scriptures. Without question, Paul's use of this terminology played into the hands of those who thought that evil was somehow material and that the problem with us humans is that we are in bodies. But a careful study of Paul's writings will make it very plain that that is not what he is saying. Rather, he is talking about two attitudes. One attitude glorifies human abilities and efforts, utilizing the strategies and priorities of this world. The other attitude emphasizes the relaxing of one's own efforts and dependence on the Spirit of God to achieve His desires through us. So "the flesh" is my way of accomplishing the serious ends of salvation and success and achievement. But "the spirit" speaks of our willingness to allow the Holy One to come in His infinitely creative and incongruous ways and, with laughter, to deliver us.

Ishmael is a product of "the flesh," as Paul explains in Galatians 4:21-31. I can imagine Abraham and Sarah discussing how they could keep God's promise for Him. How can they supply their need for a son? Ah, we can work out this perfectly legal little maneuver: you can impregnate Hagar, and it will be all right. And nine months later Abraham stands before God and says, "This is the baby you promised, isn't it?" But God says, "No. That's not My son; that's your son, and because you insisted on doing it for yourself, the world will have more hell."

ACCEPTING WHAT WE HAVE NOT EARNED

But when Abraham and Sarah stood before God 14 years later with Isaac in their arms, there was no way it could be said that that was their baby. That was God's baby. He in His grace had let them bear him and share him and laugh with him and giggle over his funny antics. Of course they named him "Laughter." Grace is the opportunity to quit taking ourselves so damned seriously. Now while you are getting your eyebrows back off the ceiling, let me hasten to tell you that I did not use idle profanity in that last sentence. It is those who know they are damned and who must save themselves through their own efforts who must be serious 24 hours a day. But those who know the grace of God, who know that they are accepted, not *because* of their efforts, but *in spite* of them, can relax. In that relaxation they are able to see God where they have never seen Him before. In a flower, in a mass of clouds, in a child's face, or even in a pun, God is there. It is grace that lets us do that, because we don't have to earn everything on our own.

Sometimes we hear Christians making statements like, "I'd rather burn out for Jesus than rust out for the devil." Usually that is seen as commendable commitment, but I wonder. I wonder if it may not be a way of sanctifying our need to take care of ourselves. Maybe it's a way of expressing the belief that God can't make it without our working our fingers to the bone for Him—Christian pride.

Over against that is the simple joy of children in their instinctive acceptance of grace. I love a story that came out of the return of the hostages from Iran in 1981. Somewhere in the state of Washington they were having a celebration, and among the celebrants there was a little group of three-year-olds who had been brought from a day-care center more than 20 miles away. A reporter asked the teacher, "Why have you brought them?" The teacher replied with great seriousness, "This is an important event in these children's lives. They need to have this experience." Then the reporter said to one of the little kids, "Why are you here?" And the little guy answered with great excitement, "Because the sausages are coming home!" Beautiful! He didn't know *why* it was a big day, but it was a big day, and that was all right with him. That's grace—we don't have to explain everything or earn everything; we can accept and live with the incongruities of life and even find God in them.

GRACE AND LEISURE

What does grace have to do with leisure? I am sure you have already seen many of the implications, but let me point out a few that are of special importance. First, "Work, for the Night Is Coming," may be an expression of devotion to the God who has saved us, but it is equally likely to be an expression of our felt need to earn our way to heaven through our own efforts. Whenever our work is an effort to justify ourselves in the sight of God and of human beings, it flies directly in the face of that central Christian truth—grace.

Second, grace is the gift of receiving. United Methodist Bishop Earle Hunt tells of being treated to a lavish evening out by a parishioner in one of his first churches. The pastor and his wife were living on very little, so this entertainment meant a great deal to them. Hunt says that he just fell over himself all evening trying to express his thanks. Finally, the by-now somewhat exasperated parishioner said, "Son, you're going to have to learn how to receive." To learn how to receive is what leisure is about. No, I don't deserve not to have to work 16 hours a day, 7 days a week, but then, neither do I deserve an eternity of glory in the presence of God. No, I don't deserve the right to reflect on the wonders of creation or on the principles of life, nor do I deserve the privilege of having several Bibles in my home. Work can be a subtle attempt to deny grace, whereas leisure can be the acceptance of the undeserved.

Third, grace is laughter, and without grace, laughter is a luxury which can ill be afforded. To be at leisure is to know that everything does not depend on you, to be able to look at all the strange things in life and to laugh, knowing that your Father can bring good out of *everything*. When I was growing up, I was always rather embarrassed by the simple silliness of my parents' Christian friends in our rural community. Now I know why they, some of whom had endured harsh tragedies and all of whom were accustomed to very hard work, could laugh so uproariously over some very simple things. There was none of the glitteringly hard "humor" of our times, none of the sly double entendre that seems to be the only thing funny in our society, none of the cutting mockery that characterizes modern comedians. No, these were people whose experience of the grace of God had freed them to take life as they found it and to find joy in one another and in all the crazy things that happened around them. If you ever want to hear innocent laughter, listen to a group of Christians who really know the grace of God.

A life in which there is no leisure is very likely to be a life that has yet some distance to go in experiencing God's grace.

N I N E

FREEDOM

In his book *A Theology of Play*, Jurgen Moltmann says, "Our existence is justified and made beautiful before we are able to do, or fail to do, anything." What does that mean? It means that accomplishing something or failing to accomplish something doesn't make our existence more or less justified or beautiful. When our labor is successful, joy was already there before we began. When we have failed, the true source of our being remains unchanged. In that knowledge is freedom, the freedom of knowing that we are accepted by God.

Freedom is the partner of grace. Since our relationship with God is secured by grace, we are free from the need to prove ourselves. Because God's love is given, not earned, we are free to enjoy it to the full. This means that if biblical religion is about anything, it is about freedom. Remember the freedom of the Garden of Eden: "You are free to eat from any tree in the garden" (Gen. 2:16, NIV). There were limits—but what wide limits! Within the boundary of a single act of submission to their Creator, our first mother and father had incredible freedom, the freedom to explore, to use, to develop, to discover, to enjoy. That was the kind of freedom our Father intended for us to know.

THE LIMITS TIGHTENED BY SIN

We have lost that primeval freedom. In their refusal to acknowledge their dependency, Adam and Eve planted a seed of rebellion in the hearts of all their children. That rebellion now makes us focus on what we *cannot* do rather than on what we *can* do. That rebellion makes us direct our energy to destroying limits. It is precisely because of those tendencies that the boundaries have had to be narrowed around us. We are like the child who insists on climbing the back fence. Not only will that fence probably be raised, the child may very well be made to stay in the house where his mother can watch him. The freedom of the yard has been lost because he refuses to live within that freedom.

So there comes to the race the experience of bondage, as typified by the bondage of the Hebrew people in Egypt. On this point it is necessary to thread our way carefully between two equally dangerous reefs. On one side looms the suggestion that the sole purpose of the story of the deliverance from Egypt is to illustrate the freedom from the spiritual bondage of sin that Christ's death on the cross makes possible. But this thought plays far too easily into the hands of the world's oppressors who seek to keep their people in political bondage. The weight of the Old Testament passages that promise deliverance from physical bondage argues against this idea. God intends for His people to be free, and this includes political freedom.

Another reef looms on the other side, and its breakers are very near the contemporary church. This is the idea that the Bible's view of freedom is *primarily* political. In this view, the fact that the preponderance of Old Testament promises of deliverance relate to deliverance from political oppression means that political freedom is central to biblical thought. Since it is central, the argument goes, any means is justifiable to achieve it. Unfortunately this concept plays into the hands of revolutionary groups whose goals and methods are anything but Christian.

In my opinion, this latter view misses the clear thrust of the whole Bible. Yes, it is plain that God's design is for His people to know political freedom, but that is not His chief goal. His chief goal is that they might know eternal life and the freedom that that brings. No reading of the New Testament can fail to make this clear. Jesus was not the political Messiah the Jews mistakenly expected. To subordinate His teachings on personal and community righteousness to the achievement of political goals is a misappropriation of His words.

FREEDOM IS GOD'S IDEA

But with these understandings in mind, it is plain that freedom for His people is God's intent. The Passover? Freedom from Egypt, yes, but also from the curse of death. "Why do we keep this Passover, Father? Because we're not slaves anymore!" The Torah? Freedom from the blindness of ignorance. Who is so bound as the person who does not know God's way? The cross? Freedom from the condemnation of a broken law. Thank God, His law, which is so good, so beautiful, so true—and so damning—need damn me no longer. I'm free, not *from* the law, but from the condemnation *of* the law. The Holy Spirit? Free from the need to earn my continuing sonship by labored obedience, free to live a righteous life in His glorious strength. Freedom! "You will know the truth and the truth will set you free. ... If the Son sets you free, you will be free indeed" (John 8:32, 36, NIV). That is the ruling thought of Christianity, the religion of freedom.

How easily we slip into the imperative mood in our Christianity. "I'm free in Christ; therefore I *must* . . ." This is the contradiction Paul addresses in his letter to the Galatians. If we are free in Christ, there are *no* actions we *must* perform (Gal. 3:1-5). Without doubt, the apostle is speaking in broad strokes here. Obviously, there are such things as duty and responsibility. In Galatians 5:14, Paul speaks of the command to love, for instance. Still duty and the responsibility must be lived out in an atmosphere of freedom.

I think there are two reasons the message of Galatians is so important to the Christian faith. The first was alluded to in the previous chapter. We have to be constantly reminded that we cannot earn our right relationship with God. This was the case with the Galatians. They started out by being saved through faith alone. They had admitted to themselves and the world that there was nothing they could do to earn God's forgiveness and the assurance of eternal life. But that is so hard for the human ego to accept. We want to deserve what we get. So the Galatians had swallowed the suggestion that while *getting* salvation was free, *keeping* it depended on their efforts. Paul insists that we get *and* keep salvation by faith alone. Yes, he wants to avoid any suggestion of license (Gal. 5:16-24), but he sees the subtle suggestion that Christians can keep themselves saved by works as being equally as dangerous as license. "It is for freedom that Christ has set us free" (Gal. 5:1, NIV).

The second reason it is so important that our Christian lives be lived in an atmosphere of freedom is that there is implicit in the imperative (I must) that blurring of means and ends we have talked about before in this book. The imperative suggests that I must do "this" in order to have or achieve "that." It doesn't have to be that way, but it frequently is. The result is that "this" becomes devalued because I am doing it to get "that," and "that" is what really matters.

WHAT *REALLY* MATTERS?

Let me illustrate from the life of a pastor. How easily a pastor comes to feel that he or she must visit a certain number of people each week in order to be a successful pastor! What's the end here, the really valuable thing? It is being a successful pastor, isn't it? The pastor's encounters with people then become a means to an end, with the end being success. The visits themselves and to a significant extent the people themselves have no value. They have become a means. Whenever a thing becomes a means, it is very difficult to enjoy it for itself.

I remember the struggles my seminary students had with this issue when they attempted to minister to the aged and infirm. "Did I really minister to that old lady? All I could do was to be with her and hold her hand. I couldn't share the Gospel with her; I couldn't help her with her problems; I'm not sure she even knew I was there. Was that ministry?" "Ministry," and a certain concept of ministry, had become an imperative. Because of that, the idea of simply being with someone in the name of Christ became of no value. Those fledgling pastors had to justify their existence. It is hard to be free enough to really hear Christ's words, "Inasmuch as you did it to the least of these ..."

This idea that some things are valuable and other things merely useful goes against the grain of the doctrine of creation. In creation all things are valuable in themselves. I say to God, "Why did You make mosquitoes?" God replies, "Because I wanted to. Is that OK?" "No, not exactly. It's okay that You made collie dogs; I like collie dogs, but I don't like mosquitoes. They don't serve my purposes." Suppose God said, "I just like the way they go 'bazooooom' when they fly." Would that be all right? I wonder.

THE FREEDOM OF PLAY

Christianity is about freedom, our freedom in Christ to be ourselves and to value things for themselves. But where is there a possibility of expressing that Christian freedom in life? Where can you do that? Where can we be free to some extent of the world of imperatives? One answer is, in play. Play is the place where you can do something with seriousness and with purpose and yet the outcome doesn't really matter. It is not imperative, or it ought not to be imperative, who wins. So then the game, the project, the thought, becomes an end in itself. Why do I sit down with my three children to play a board game? I usually ask myself that about halfway through the game! Why am I doing this? There they are, jumping around, throwing the dice at each other, and I think, *Why? Oh well, they'll learn good sportsmanship.* Really? More likely they'll learn how to lose badly! No, I really do it because it's fun, and it gives me a chance to do something with my kids.

The great value of play is that in itself this experience is free. They don't have to do it; I don't have to do it. We're here to be free. Is it possible that playing a game is the most Christian thing I've done all day? Possibly. In an activity that is not required we express the divine truth that there is nothing we *have* to do to justify ourselves in the sight of God except to receive His free provision. Leisure is not merely a momentary break until we can get back to that truly Christian activity—our work—but it is a vital expression of the truth that we are free in Christ.

THE LEISURE CRISIS

THE FREEDOM OF THE SABBATH

This concept of Christian freedom relates to our concept of
the Sabbath. I know that we Christians do not keep the
Sabbath. But to me there is a good deal of sloppy thinking
on this issue. Two things are obvious for us Christians. We
don't make Saturday our day of rest and celebration. Why?
For the same reason that we don't keep the Passover but do
observe Communion. Something has happened that doesn't
do away with the old observance but instead gives it a
whole new meaning. Deliverance from death has taken on a
whole new significance for us. All that was true of the old
idea has been preserved, but new realities have made the
meaning deeper.

The same thing has happened to the old concept of one
day when we remind ourselves that all of our time is God's,
that we are not the source of our subsistence, and that we
belong to Him. All of those things remain true, but something more has been added. On the first day of the week our
freedom from the curse of death broke forth. Likewise, it
was on the first day of the week that the long-awaited
promise of the Father—the Holy Spirit—broke loose upon
God's children. Three approaches can be taken in the light
of these events. One is a simple repudiation of the "Jewish"
idea (after all, we are Christians). This would say that
Sunday should be like any other day. But the theological
truths that the observance of a day set apart from all the
rest teaches are as essential for Christians as they were for
any Israelite.

Another approach may be called the "Puritan" one. We
merely overlay the Old Testament demands with a new
Christian superstructure. Unfortunately, this means that the
Sabbath is primarily seen as the time when you can't do this
and you can't do that and you can't do the other thing. It
becomes a time of bondage rather than a time of freedom.

But there is yet a third approach. In this approach we see the essential meaning of *Sabbath* as being as vital for us today as ever, but we realize the truth that the Jews of Jesus' day had lost sight of. The observation of a day apart is *for* us, not against us. The Sabbath is not the time when we can't, but rather the time when we can. This is a day when we must not work, but that is so that we will be reminded that we are free, forced to be free, if you will. God requires that we will be at leisure!

This means that far from Sunday being a time *not* to play, it is precisely a time *to* play. To be sure, there are behaviors that express freedom but contradict Christian principles. Leisure that is merely self-indulgence is hardly a statement of our freedom in Christ. By the same token, I think diversion through commercial sports on Sunday has very little part in an expression of Christian freedom. On the other hand, a family football game has everything to commend it.

What all this means then is that Christian freedom is not so much freedom *from* but freedom *to*—freedom to value, freedom to be, freedom to enjoy, freedom to try on. So much of play is trying on. Here we are free to be without being overly worried about conventional societal pressures. What about it? Would I like being Simon Legree? Would I like sticking somebody now that I've got Boardwalk and Park Place? Would I like bankrupting my kids? Here is the freedom to explore that question, who am I? Is this who I am?

THE FREEDOM OF LOVE

I think you see this truth of Christian freedom best in the story of Mary pouring out the costly perfume on Jesus' feet (John 12:1-8). "What a dumb woman," say the disciples.

"She obviously doesn't know how much that stuff is worth. She's wasted it." No, what she has done is an expression of freedom. She does know how much it's worth, but its real worth is as an expression of her delight in Jesus, her love for Him. A useless act, and yet not useless at all. I love the way Jesus responds to the charges that Mary should have done something "useful" with the perfume. He says, "Well, you want this to be a useful gesture? OK, I'll make it useful. She's anointing Me for My burial. Does that make it OK now?" I think irony just drips from His words. The value of Mary's act is not its usefulness. The value of it is what it is in itself. Love does not have to justify itself. Love is free. As leisure enables us to learn that truth and enjoy our freedom in Christ, leisure is a benefit to our Christian growth.

T E N

WORSHIP

osef Pieper, in his book *Leisure: The Basis of Culture*, says what appears to be a very strange thing. He says that worship is at the heart of a right concept and use of leisure. My first reaction to that is, *what in the world does worship have to do with leisure?* Of course worship is a good thing, but it seems pretty far removed from leisure.

The definition of leisure Pieper is working with is that of Aristotle, which we talked about at the beginning of this book. He is not thinking of mere diversion or entertainment; he is thinking of time when we are free to let our minds and spirits loose to realize the possibilities inherent in them. In that light his statement begins to make a little more sense.

Another important point is his understanding of worship. He shows that the Old English root word for our modern word *worship* is *worth-ship*. It is in the context of and the expression of our faith that we define our whole system of values—what is worthwhile to us. Nor is this interesting root connection merely accidental; it's not a pun. In just the same way, the English word *culture* originally referred to that which springs from cults, that which springs from worship. In other words, it was worship that produced the finest in art and music and literature. The church gave gifted people the leisure to write and compose and paint, and it supplied them with a system of values and a reason to concentrate their abilities in order to achieve excellence.

WORSHIP GIVES MEANING

Now Pieper's point becomes clearer. Without the unifying value of genuine worship, life is without meaning. Who wants to look at the world and understand how things fit together and where the ultimate meanings lie if there is no meaning? Without ultimate meaning, culture, creativity, expressiveness, contemplation, and putting the world together make no sense.

That is what we see around us at every turn. For most of our contemporaries there is no unifying principle in the world. There is no meaning to life. Why would you want to study botany? There is no meaning in the organization of the plant. There *appears* to be some meaning, but that is the bad joke of human existence: there appears to be meaning in life when in fact there is none. It is no wonder that much of leisure today has become mere mindless diversion, canned entertainment, or activities centered on the consumption of alcohol.

So what Pieper is saying is that unless you have what worship gives, a belief that there is meaning in life, there is no point in developing your spirit or your mind. You had better unplug them, because they're just going to cause you a lot of grief. You're liable to be seduced by the idea of meaning and try to find it when in fact there is none.

CELEBRATE!

But just what is worship and what does it do? What are we really doing when we ascribe ultimate worth to God? A glance at the Psalms, the hymnbook of the church, may help us at this point. First and foremost we find praise and celebration.

Praise the Lord!
Praise, O servants of the Lord,
Praise the name of the Lord!
Blessed be the name of the Lord
From this time forth and forevermore!
From the rising of the sun to its going down
The Lord's name is to be praised.

(Ps. 113:1-3, NKJV)

This note of praise can be heard again and again in the Psalms. What is its source? It arises from a profound sense of wonder and gratitude at the nature and character of God. The psalmists are overwhelmed by the truth that this God who has revealed Himself to them, who is the Creator of all things, is so good and so kind, so willing to save His creatures from traps of their own making, so ready to meet the lowliest with complete humility. That is cause for celebration! Think what the ultimate power in the universe could be like. He could be a monster. But He isn't. He is good. Praise His name! The great missionary E. Stanley Jones has a line in one of his books that fits at this point. He says that he is like the man who found the expensive pearl in Jesus' parable (Matt. 13:45-46). At an early age he gave all that he had in exchange for Jesus, and he has been hugging himself with delight ever since at the great deal he got. That's cause for celebration!

But what does celebration have to do with leisure? Everything, when what we are celebrating is the freedom and joy that is ours because we know that our Creator's response to us is grace. If in fact we have learned to worship Him in praise and celebration, then all of life is an adventure. No longer is it a grim mounting up of accomplishments to demonstrate—to ourselves most of all—that we are persons of worth. As the hymnwriter says, "This is my Father's world; He shines in all that's fair." If we have come to know that in celebration and praise, then the whole world is a treasure house, a wondrous place to explore and to contemplate, all the while knowing that again and again, when we least expect it, Father's laughing face is going to be looking out at us. We need worship in order to develop that sense of wonder and delight in God.

ADMITTING OUR NEED FOR GOD

A second characteristic of worship as it appears in the Psalms is the admission of dependence. Again and again the psalmists declare their absolute need for God. Consider for instance Psalm 27.

One thing I have desired of the Lord,
That will I seek:
That I may dwell in the house of the Lord
All the days of my life,
To behold the beauty of the Lord,
And to inquire in His temple.
For in the time of trouble
He shall hide me in His pavilion;
In the secret place of His tabernacle
He shall hide me;
He shall set me high upon a rock.

(Ps. 27:4-5, NKJV)

To admit that we are totally dependent on God and to celebrate that fact is one of the most concrete ways to declare to the world that He is God and we are not. It is the way we demonstrate just how much He is worth in our scheme of things. If in fact our worship is really a means of putting God in our debt, a way of showing Him how much He needs us, then we have not worshiped Him at all. We have tried to manipulate Him, to work a deal with Him, but we have not worshiped. This is why God invites us to bring Him our petitions and supplications (Phil. 4:6). We are confessing that we cannot take care of ourselves, but He can.

If we have never learned this lesson of worship, leisure will come very hard for us. We will not have time to quit taking care of ourselves. We will not be able to lay aside our efforts and rejoice in the delicious relief of doing nothing but reclining in the arms of God. Again the hymnwriter says it best: "Oh, to lie forever here, doubt and care and self resign, while He whispers in my ear—I am His and He is mine." The person who has learned this truth knows the secret of ceasing from his own works and entering into rest (Heb. 4:10).

OUR WORSHIP IS VALUABLE

There is one more element of worship that is important to the issue of leisure—the worth of the worshiper. Again, this is a characteristic of the Psalms. What the worshiper has to offer God is of value. The worshiper is not just a cog in a machine, not just one drop of water lost in an ocean. He or she is a person, made in the image of *the* Person. Our praise, our delight, our glad admission of dependence is of significance precisely because it is freely given.

When I consider Your heavens, the work of Your
  fingers,
The moon and the stars, which You have ordained,
What is man that You are mindful of him,

And the son of man that You visit him?
For You have made him a little lower than the angels,
And You have crowned him with glory and honor.

(Ps. 8:3-5, NKJV)

This is worship, a free act of obedience given by one who could withhold it. The importance of this idea for leisure is that those who have this significance and importance are able to contemplate their world and reflect on it, to follow in their maker's footsteps and be creative, to take charge of time that is not required for necessary activities, and to find their significance not in production but in relationships.

On reflection, I think we can see that Pieper is exactly right, that culture, the idea of the unified world that has meaning and significance and is worth investment in, is rooted in a leisure that springs from a celebrative, dependent, significant relationship to a Creator who has designed a world of meaning and purpose and delight.

This means that our worship should be leading us into that kind of relationship with God. If it is not leading me in that direction, then I had better check my worship. If it is not undergirding my sense of meaning and purpose and glory in life, then it's not doing what it can do.

GOOD-FOR-NOTHING WORSHIP

But as soon as I say that, I must come back to the ax I've been grinding throughout this book. I must not suggest that we should worship because it will do something for us. Worship is of value precisely when it is *useless*. Why do I worship? So my week will go well? Because God will get lonely if I don't show up to say "Hi"? No, I worship to say, "God, You are really something." I worship to say, "You're valuable." I worship to say, "God, You're worth everything I've got." It's "worth-ship," remember? Of course, I need to be very careful what my worship practices say about God's worth. If I say as though it were a big deal, "God, You're worth one hour a week," somehow I don't imagine God getting terribly excited about my worship. It sounds as though I'm trying to use Him, giving Him what I consider to be the minimum necessary for services desired.

No, as Moltmann says, "so long as religion and God serve some purpose outside of themselves, they themselves are not necessary." If I serve God in order to succeed, then succeeding is important, and God is but a means. In the same way, if I serve God in order to be saved, then being saved is important and God is a means to that good end.

That's not worship; it's idolatry. In his classic definition, St. Augustine defines idolatry as the worship of what should be used and the use of what should be worshiped. When I make God a means, I make Him into an idol. I have made Him useful. Worship is the experience of enjoying God, not using Him. We are called, as the Westminster Confession says, to enjoy Him forever. Just to enjoy Him.

For most churchgoers this idea that we go to church in order to enjoy God is pretty theoretical. Most of us, I imagine, would respond to a question about why we attend church with some version of "Because of what I get out of it." When we ask someone why they changed churches, the frequent answer is, "Well, I just wasn't getting anything out of it." What are we saying by such a statement? Are we not saying that we worship because it is useful to us?

Compare that to the responses of a young man who is deeply in love. Ask him why he goes on a date with his girlfriend. What will he say? Will he say, "Because of what I get out of it"? Not likely. He will probably say something like, "I just like to be with her." Will the date be "good for anything"? Oh yes, it may help them to know each other a little better, but that isn't the reason they do it. They do it purely and simply because they enjoy being together.

That's what the experience of worship is meant to be—a time to enjoy God without distraction, a time to bask in His presence. Maybe sometimes when a person says, "I didn't get anything out of it," they are really saying, "I didn't experience the joy of the presence of God here." There may be a number of reasons for that lack. Maybe we are simply caught up in the repetition of forms (and some of the least liturgical churches are as caught up in the repetition of forms as any of their liturgical counterparts). Or maybe there is so much theological ambiguity that none of us in the church really know what we believe. Or maybe there is so much emphasis on the sermon (have you ever heard everything in the service before the sermon referred to as "the preliminaries"?) which is so shallow or overly cognitive or judgmental that the true God couldn't break into the place with a pickax.

This is not to suggest that we all have to hire showmen instead of pastors, people who will manage our "worship productions" rather than shepherds who will die for their flocks. That sort of thing is ultimately as damaging to a true enjoyment of God as the opposite. Just because someone has enjoyed the entertainment is no proof that they have worshiped God. In fact, they may gain such a tinsel-bedecked view of Him that they will never be able to see Him as He really is in His majesty, His holiness, and His awe-ful greatness.

So let's not emphasize human satisfaction over divine encounter, nor trappings over reality. At the same time let's keep before our eyes that the purpose of worship is not to lay on people some profound theological truth, to equip them for ministry, to prick their social consciences, or to help them have a greater sense of self-worth, as good as all those ends are. The end of worship is God, nothing more and nothing less. If in the encounter with God those other things happen, as they certainly will, fine, but God Himself is the end. We do not worship to get or to prove or to learn. We worship to be free and at rest in His presence. When that happens, we will become interested in God's Word for its own sake, because of who He is and what He's made. Again, we can hear our young friend thinking about a date say, "Gee, I don't care what we do or where we go. I just want to be with her."

WE NEED ONE ANOTHER

We need to recognize something else about worship. From a biblical point of view the enjoyment of God cannot adequately take place in isolation. It must be in a body of believers. The whole concept of worship that we find in that sentimental hymn pollsters tell us is an all-time favorite of American Christians, "In the Garden," is badly one-sided. Yes, God does relate to us as individuals, and we *can* know Him privately. But according to both the Old and the New Testaments, the main context for worship is a community of believers.

In that community I come with brothers and sisters of like mind focused on the glory and wonder, the majesty and power, the goodness and purity, the love and holiness of God, and in a sense of awe and wonder and delight we can say, "God, You are worthy of our worship." This experience does several things for us related to leisure. First of all this need to be with others, to submit our desires to theirs in some degree, will remind us that we are not self-sufficient, that alone we cannot determine the course of our own existence. It will also help us to recognize that we do not have a corner on all the truth. Our views are one-sided and need the correction of our sisters and brothers. This humility is fundamental to leisure, where we can cease from our own efforts and learn to accept and receive.

ABUNDANCE

Finally there is in worship the experience of abundance: abundance of grace, abundance of life, abundance of joy, abundance of provision. That abundance makes it possible for me to value things for themselves rather than for what they can do for me. When I have more than enough, then I can quit being eaten up with the drive to justify my own existence. I can relax, accept God's provision, and enjoy Him. When I have come to that point, I can begin to enjoy my own existence. When I can value God for Himself, then I can know that I am a creature of that God, and I can thank God for myself. I can thank God for what He has brought into my life, and in Moltmann's words, enter into a calm rejoicing in existence itself.

We come back, then, to Pieper's idea. Yes, worship is essential to leisure. When we have experienced to the depths of our beings the reality of our Father's love for us, His ability to care for us, His abundant provision for us, and the pure joy of resting in His presence, then we will be able to be free from the tyrannical side of the work ethic. We will be able to value His world for itself, not merely for what it can do for us. We will be able to receive without asking whether we have earned it all. We won't need to escape from our minds in our free time, nor will we need to escape the drudgery of our days in more goods-consumptive and exotic entertainment. We will have learned how to be at leisure.

E L E V E N

THE CHRISTIAN'S CALLING

We have been talking about biblical principles that relate to leisure. So far we have talked about creation, grace, freedom, and worship. The fifth and final principle rests on and sums up the previous four. This is the biblical understanding of the Christian's calling. What are we called to? What is it God wants for us; what is it He has in mind for us? These questions are significant for leisure because they speak to the most appropriate use of our time. If God's purpose for us is accomplishment, that says one thing about our time. If that is not God's purpose, then we need a different way of looking at our time.

In my opinion the clearest and most concise source for this biblical understanding of God's intent for His people is in the second and the third chapters of Paul's letter to the Colossians. In this passage Paul gets at, more explicitly than any place else in the Scriptures, what it is we are called to.

From what appears in the book, it has been concluded that Paul was in prison in Rome at the time of the book's writing. He had been visited by Epaphras, who exercised spiritual leadership in the Colossian church (1:7), and had evidently learned from Epaphras of some problems that were surfacing in that church.

THE COLOSSIANS' QUESTION

From Paul's teaching in this letter, we may deduce that the problems revolved around two differing answers to the question of Christian calling. On the one hand were those holding a position similar to that of Aquinas and Descartes. To those of this position the thing that best characterizes human beings is thought. Thus, those who held this view at Colossae believed that it is what you know that makes you a Christian.

Unfortunately, the teachings these people thought Christians should know were heretical! They believed that there was a special, secret knowledge which only the privileged few got to learn. Recent findings at Nag Hammadi in Egypt have generally confirmed the outlines of these teachings as they have been pieced together from various early sources, including such rebuttals of them as are found in the Book of Colossians. Because these people put such an emphasis on knowledge, they have come to be called "Gnostics," from the Greek word for knowledge, *gnosis*.

THE KNOWING GNOSTICS

Among other things, the Gnostics believed that the cosmos was dualistic, with an eternal struggle going on between good spirit and evil matter. They also believed that there was a progression of beings called aeons coming from God, with each succeeding one getting a little less like Him. Far down in the chain, one of the aeons produced a being known as the Demiurge. This being, who was almost, but not quite, wholly evil, created the earth. At some point one of the higher aeons fell and became imprisoned in matter. He longed to return to pure spirituality but could not. So the most perfect aeon came to earth and after many sufferings led the fallen aeon back up the chain to pure spirituality. If we human beings could be initiated into that secret knowledge, learning how the Redeemer progressed back up through the chain, we could do the same thing. At all points along the way the soul is opposed by the lower aeons, so the special knowledge consists of special names and passwords, sealings, holy foods, and so on. Doesn't this sound a great deal like "Dungeons and Dragons"? There really is nothing new under the sun, is there?

Over against all of this is the Christian revelation. There is only one eternal principle, not two as the Gnostics believed. He is the Creator, and He is wholly good. The material creation is not evil. It became corrupted through the efforts of a fallen creature who was motivated by pride, but that creature did not himself corrupt the world. It was corrupted because of free human choice as a result of temptation by that creature. Our bodies are not evil. In fact, we will have bodies in heaven. Wouldn't that make a Gnostic shrivel up? Also, the Saviour did not come to save the cosmos; He came to save sinners. And we are saved simply by accepting what He has done for us. There are no final exams to pass after death. Praise God—no passwords to know, no secret names to remember. It's all free. In fact, after all the final exams I've had to suffer through, if I discover that I have another to face after death, I'll know I've been lost after all!

I am fascinated by the way Paul approaches this problem in his letter. He does not leave the truth undefended. Especially in the first chapter, he makes it very plain who God is and who Christ is and how salvation is received. But when he really begins to lay into the Gnostics in 2:8 and following, he does not so much say that their problem is the wrong knowledge as that it is knowledge itself: "Beware lest anyone cheat you through philosophy and empty deceit, according to the tradition of men, according to the basic principles of the world, and not according to Christ" (NKJV).

Paul does not say that the problem with the Gnostics is that they are peddling the *wrong* philosophy, but that they are peddling philosophy! He doesn't say that what these folks are teaching is bad. He simply dismisses their whole approach. Knowing the names of angels? He doesn't say, "You don't have to know the names of angels, but you do have to know something else." He says it isn't what you know that makes you a Christian.

Now that's pretty scary. I've spent my whole life trying to figure out what I need to know to be a good Christian. Of course, this is not to say that Paul is dismissing all doctrine. Far from it—you only have to read the Book of Romans to know that's not the case. Christianity is not an irrational religion; it is a religion that appeals to the mind. But Paul is dealing here with the point of view that says, "I am what I know, and because I know a lot, I am somebody." Paul is vehemently denying that view. We are who we are in Christ. "For in Him dwells all the fullness of the Godhead bodily; and you are complete in Him, who is the head of all principality and power" (2:9-10, NKJV). All my knowledge is good, but if I think it gives me special standing with God, I am badly mistaken.

THE DOING JUDAIZERS

The other group of people in the Colossian church would have been followers of Luther and Marx. What is our calling? Our calling is to be doers, workers. These were the

Judaizers. The Judaizers were saying that it's not what you
know that makes so much difference, but it's what you do.
You must follow certain standards and achieve certain
goals: you have to be circumcised; you have to eat the right
things; you have to drink the right things; you have to go to
the right number of services at the right times; you have to
have the right kind of devotions. It's what you do that
makes you who you are.

Nor is this merely an old Judaistic problem. It is as much
a problem today as ever. How do I know I'm a Christian?
Love? Oh, that's so intangible. Kindness, justice, patience?
Well, how do I know I really do have those qualities? How
much easier it is to measure my religion by the tangibles:
what I drink, what I wear, what I drive. These days, of
course, things have gotten tangled up. It used to be that I
could prove I was a Christian because I *didn't* drive a
luxury car. Now I can prove I'm a Christian with God's
blessing because I *do* drive a luxury car. But in either case,
the principle is the same: I'm a Christian because of what I
do or don't do, what I have or don't have.

Paul's response to all of this is unequivocal. I wonder if
he could get away with it in most of our churches.

Let no one pass judgment on you in questions of food
and drink or with regard to a festival or a new moon or
a Sabbath. . . . Let no one disqualify you, insisting on
self-abasement and worship of angels, taking his stand
on visions, puffed up without reason by his sensuous
mind (2:16, 18, RSV).

Wow! I'm afraid a good part of the evangelical movement
wouldn't have made it under those guidelines. We've spent
our lives passing judgment on people with regard to questions of food and drink and festivals. We've spent our lives
disqualifying people because they didn't have the right
kinds of devotions.

The most telling thing he can say, though, is in the twenty-third verse of the second chapter. He is talking now about both knowing and doing, and he says, "These have indeed an appearance of wisdom in promoting rigor of devotion and self-abasement and severity to the body, but they are of no value in checking the indulgence of the flesh" (RSV). Wow, again! He says that I can know all kinds of things, and I can be a terrific worker, and yet somehow those don't touch who I am. All of us know the reality of that. All of us have known Christian workers who could work rings around anybody and have worked themselves into a coronary. All of us have known of men who could put an arrow in the eye of a fly at fifty paces, doctrinally speaking, and have left their wives to run off with their secretaries. Paul is right. Our Christianity must go deeper than either knowing or doing if it is to touch the core of our being, the root of our actions.

CALLED TO BE

So what *is* our calling? If our calling is not first of all to be thinkers—and please hear me again, I'm not dismissing that; as an educator, it's my business—and if our calling is not to be workers—and I'm not dismissing that; it is part of what we are as human beings—what are we? Paul's answer is that it is not what we know; it is not what we do; it is what we *are* that makes us Christian. We are called to *be* something first, not to know something or do something. This is why the apostle says, "Look, put off that stuff. You're dead. You're dead with Christ. So don't get tangled up with the earthly stuff, the worldly stuff" (2:20–3:3, *my paraphrase*).

My grandmother was a saint in every sense of the word, and yet she was very worldly. She didn't know it, but she was. She was very hung up on skirt length. She was very hung up on hairstyle. Paul says that's being worldly. She would have died if I had ever called her worldly. She was *not* worldly; that's why her skirts were so long. She was *not* worldly; that's why she wore her hair in a bun. Paul said, "You're hung up on this world."

But if that is so, what is to prevent us from taking off that skirt that's down to our ankles and putting on hot pants? If it's worldly to be concerned about externals, why shouldn't we just live in any way we please? That brings us to Paul's central point. What makes us Christian is our identification with Christ.

> If then you were raised with Christ, seek those things which are above, where Christ is, sitting at the right hand of God. . . . For you died, and your life is hidden with Christ in God. When Christ who is our life appears, then you also will appear with Him in glory (3:1, 3-4, NKJV).

If we're Christians, says Paul, something has happened to our being. We have become one with Christ. It is this alone that saves us. It is not what we know or what we do; it is our relationship to the Lord. If we have that relationship, it will produce a desire to know and a desire to do, but the relationship is primary, and the behaviors are secondary. Before we are called to know or do, we must *be*. Our human way is to try to produce the relationship by what we know or do. That's backward from God's way.

BEING LIKE JESUS

I'm fascinated by the way Paul develops this point. In the first half of Colossians 3 he says in effect, "Put those worldly attitudes to death. Since you're dead in Christ, don't focus on the earthly side of things. What you need to do is to put to death those attitudes that are the real problem:

lust, greed, selfish anger, deception. Instead, you need to put on, then..." Now there are two things that catch my eye here. First of all, notice that he is telling a corpse to die! "Since you're dead, now die!" How strange! What he is saying is this: the key to victory in the Christian life is not to know more or to try harder. Rather the key is that total surrender that will make it possible for what is already ours implicitly because of our relationship to Christ to become explicit. The key is not more struggle, but greater surrender.

Second, notice what it is we are to put on when the old ways have been put off through God's grace. They are all *qualities*. It is not doing or knowing, but being that is important to God. Notice that the first quality is compassion. The first thing He wants me to be in Christ is a person who is able to feel what other people feel. Every one of the other qualities listed exists in relation to other people too. Not one can be practiced in isolation. For instance, I have no trouble whatsoever loving my children when they are not at home. But let them walk in the door, and then the rubber hits the road. That's what Wesley meant when he said that there is no holiness except social holiness. He was not talking about what we think of as social work, though he did plenty of that. He meant that there is no holiness except that which is lived out in relation to other people.

So when I stand before the bar of heaven, God is not going to ask me, "John, what did you do?" or, "John, tell me what you know." He's going to say, "John, in the 40, 50, 60, or 80 years of your life what did you become? Did you become compassionate? Did you become gentle? What did you become?" That's my calling. That's your calling. Our first calling is not to a vocation. We are not first called to be teachers or pastors or business persons or farmers or whatever. Our first calling is to be like Jesus.

I love the way the passage moves to its climax. Just as he

said, "You're dead, now die," he now says, "You're alive, now live." Something has happened already, so that I don't have to clench my fists and grit my teeth and say, "I am going to be more compassionate toward that old biddy." Instead, I believe that somehow, Lord, in You I *am* compassionate. Instead of producing compassion that I do not have, I release what is mine in Christ. Not my work but my receiving. From the Lord Christ, I receive the compassion that He purchased in His atonement and that He made available to me through His life. We receive Christ's life. We don't earn it and we don't produce it—we receive it. Compassion, kindness, lowliness, meekness, patience—they are all there. Paul winds up with a crescendo: "Forbearing one another and, if one has a complaint against another, forgiving each other; as the Lord has forgiven you, so you also must forgive. And above all these put on love, which binds everything together in perfect harmony" (Col. 3:13-14, RSV).

At this point the symphony begins to broaden out. It has been moving in a staccato sort of way, striking each quality. Now it becomes broader and more majestic.

And let the peace of Christ rule in your hearts, to which you were called in one body (not individually in your closet), and be thankful. Let the word dwell richly, abundantly, superfluously, as you teach and admonish one another, as you sing, as you're thankful; and in whatever you do in word or deed, do everything in the name of the Lord Jesus (3:15-17, *my paraphrase*).

What is the picture here as this symphony of Paul's comes to its close? It's a kind of festival, I think, where people are admonishing one another in love; where people are singing songs and hymns and spiritual songs; where they're thanking God for one another and thanking one another for God, and doing it all in the name of Jesus. They are a people who are free, free in their love for one another and for Christ. There is no hierarchy of the knowers and the doers; there is only the unity of those who are being made one because they are all becoming like Christ.

CALLED TO LEISURE

All of this says that whatever enables us to cease from our own efforts and frees us to concentrate on what we are becoming is of tremendous benefit to us. Of course, this is exactly what the leisure we have been describing makes possible for us. Leisure is that active rest that enables us to step back a pace from the nose-to-the-grindstone sort of life and cultivate those qualities that are Christ's. Instead of focusing on our accomplishments in work or in learning, we are enabled to focus on things outside of ourselves. We are enabled to remember that it is not what we achieve but what we have received that makes us Christian. It gives us a chance to do something for itself alone and in the process to learn again to value being more than utility.

This festival Paul is describing in the third chapter of Colossians is a most appropriate point on which to draw this section. This is so because it sums up so much of what we have talked about. There is creativity in the variety of psalms and hymns and spiritual songs. There is grace, the grace of Christ which is the very cause of the celebration. There is freedom, that freedom that allows each person to contribute in his or her own way. There is obviously worship, that celebration of the nature and character of a God who values people for themselves alone and who calls them to the enjoyment of His world and of one another. Does the Bible have anything to say about leisure? Absolutely! Its central doctrines point to the necessity of leisure if we are to realize the full possibilities that are ours in Christ. Leisure is not just permissible; it is vital.

PART FOUR

WHERE TO NOW?

T W E L V E

LEISURE AND YOU

Throughout this book we have considered ways the truths we have discovered about leisure could apply to our lives. No doubt you have already thought of many applications I have not even mentioned. But I want to make the applications very specific, first for us as individuals and then for the church. This is where the real validity of what we have been discussing will have to be seen. Can we translate into life the biblical values? I am confident that we can, and that as we do, the new opportunities our culture presents to us will be a source of blessing rather than a curse.

WHERE ARE WE NOW?

As a first step in translating the truth into practice, I would like you to fill out an inventory based on the principles we have discussed in the previous chapters. It will give you a chance to look carefully at yourself in preparation for responding to the suggestions I will make in this chapter.

Answer the questions as candidly as you can, knowing that your acceptance with God does not depend on how well you answer a set of questions! Use the space provided or a separate sheet of paper for your answers.

My purpose in raising these questions is not to elevate anyone's guilt quotient. Most of us struggle with more guilt than we can handle anyway. I simply offer them to you as a means of beginning to come to grips with where you are and where you may need to begin in finding a healthy balance of work and leisure in your life. How each of us answers the questions will be different, and that's OK. This is not like an examination, where the best people get 100 points and the worst people get 32, so please don't look at it that way. This is simply a vehicle for sorting out where we are as opposed to where we want to be.

LEISURE AND YOU
A Personal Inventory
1. Why do I work?

2. What really motivates me?

3. Who am I becoming? What do I like about that and what do I not like?

4. Where on my list of priorities is the development of me as a human being in Christ?

5. In what ways do I now model grace and freedom?

6. Do I feel guilty about taking time off from work? If so, why?

7. When do I feel that my time is my own?

8. How dependent am I on goods in my leisure time?

9. Are the following playing a role in my free time at present? In what way?
   a. Expression of freedom in Christ

   b. Release from drivenness

   c. Discovery of the world about me

   d. Development of mind and spirit

   e. Expression of creativity

   f. Silence

g. Fellowship

h. Participation

WHY DO I WORK?

Let's talk about the issues the first question raises. What is the fundamental reason for my working? Am I driven to it? Do I enjoy it? Do I feel guilty if I don't work? As we have seen, there are some positive reasons for working. If we work as an expression of our commitment to God, that's positive. If we work as a means of using our gifts for the support of our family, that's positive. So also is work positive when it grows out of a desire to make a contribution, however large or small, to the society of which I am a part. In all of these, work remains a means. I can do it or not do it without affecting my fundamental being.

The problem comes when we become inseparable from our work. Then we're no longer working to live, but living to work. We may be working because we need to prove ourselves, or because we feel insignificant if we don't "make a contribution." Or we may be working to earn God's favor. In each of these the work has become a way of justifying our existence. So long as we have attitudes like these, any real leisure will be very difficult for us.

What needs to take place in us if we are working for these less than positive reasons? First of all, the very act of facing the situation is a giant step forward. Second, we need to read through Galatians and hear the message of grace. Third, we need to repent of our efforts to justify ourselves. Fourth, we need to take the situation by the throat and begin to consciously scale back those efforts. This applies as much to church work as it does to anything else. "But if I don't do it, nobody else will" is a trap. Maybe the reason they haven't done it yet is that you've been so effectively hogging the stage. Also, what does such a statement say about God? Doesn't it say that He can't accomplish His program without me? Remember His words to Elijah, when Elijah was moaning that he was the only one God had left to serve Him? "Yet I have reserved seven thousand in Israel, all whose knees have not bowed to Baal" (1 Kings 19:18, NKJV). Or think about Jesus. How easily He could have fallen into the trap of feeling that He had to reach the whole world in His lifetime, or that He had to heal all the sick or cast out all the demons! But no, He gave His time to a very limited circle of followers and frequently left the work, either by Himself or with a select few. He was a free man. He never made the mistake of confusing Himself with His work.

THE MOTIVATION FACTOR

The second question is related to the first. What is it that really motivates me? What drives me to do what I do? Is it interests? Or is it fear? Is it the satisfaction of accomplishment? Or is it inner compulsion? Am I motivated by a set of goals, or by the desire for praise, or what?

In my 23 years of schooling I turned into a pretty good student. I'm not so sure that I turned into as good a learner. I became very good at achieving course objectives. I could sort out the goals and do just as much as necessary to fully meet them. And when I had met them, I figured I was done. I tended not to ask, "Have I really developed through this? Have I really mastered this subject?" I tended to say, "I have accomplished the stated objectives of the course." And I find that pattern still in my life. I tend to be motivated in that way. I tend to want to set up some concrete objectives and to say, "Yes, I've achieved those objectives," and not ask the deeper, more intangible questions about what was really accomplished.

That question of motivation will reveal a lot to us both about our work and about our leisure. If a person has a deep need to prove himself, then both work and leisure will tend to be set up around goals and achievements. By the same token, fear of failure may very well prevent that person from trying something new in which there is a possibility of not being able to give that proof. If a person has a great need for the approval of others, she may work and avoid needed leisure because she fears that those people whose approval counts to her won't approve if she doesn't work a 60-hour week.

How shall we deal with this problem of motivation? Once again, honest appraisal of the springs of our actions is a major step. We may need to explore this with a trusted friend in order to get the needed insights, and the exercise will be a valued one for you both. If your motives are too heavily on the side of proving yourself or gaining approval (some of this is natural to all of us), reading and rereading the Song of Solomon and recognizing God's total acceptance of you with your own peculiar traits and qualities can be very helpful. Build on your own motivating factors. Use those motivations wherever possible to help you.

WHO AM I BECOMING?

This third question is a hard one. It is difficult to get a good objective look at ourselves under any circumstances, but it is especially hard when the picture we see, as here, may not be all we would like it to be. But I am not thinking of some very deep probing look, such as psychotherapy might offer.

All I am suggesting here is to take the time to honestly ask yourself, in the assurance of God's love, what is happening in your life. Interestingly enough, taking time to answer a question of this sort is one of the benefits of leisure. Most of us, I would guess, have not asked ourselves this question before now because we have never taken the time to. The useful has crowded out the necessary.

Who are you becoming? Do you like what you see? Are you more like Christ than you used to be? Are you becoming more compassionate? Are you becoming more or less people oriented?

I think in this regard of Howard Hughes, and the thought is a haunting one. Near the end of his life Hughes granted an interview, which I found very revealing. I had rather naively assumed that the man must really be miserable, hiding from people and fearful of them, but from the indications in the interview, that was not the case. When asked why he became such a recluse, he replied, "I found that people were getting in the way of my accomplishing my work, and I simply found it was a great deal more convenient not to be hampered by people bothering me." What a frightening prospect: to come to the place where people count less than work. Am I becoming the sort of person whose work is more important to me than people?

The question is not, "Am I becoming more efficient?" Nor is it, "Am I becoming more capable?" It is deeper than that. What are my manner of life, my work, my play, turning me into? For instance, how do I model grace and freedom? Do people see me as a person who is living on grace? Or do people see me as someone who makes his own way and lives on what he earns, whether money or respect? Do they see me as a free person, or do they see me as being uptight, holding all the strings of my life firmly in my hand where they demand moment-by-moment attention?

Where on my list of priorities is development of me as a person *in Christ?* We hear a lot today about personal development. I'm not really interested in self-aggrandizement and the whole "I'm going to be me and devil take the hindmost" approach. But I think there is a genuine Christian element here. "What does it profit a man to gain the whole world and lose his own soul" is still worth pondering. But what is the soul? The corresponding Hebrew word is *nephesh*, which comes very close in its range of usages to *person* or *personality* in English. It is possible to accomplish great things for God and because we have neglected to pay enough attention to the development of our own personhood to come down to the ends of our lives as persons we don't like to be with. All of our attention has been given to knowing or doing and very little to being.

GUILTY RELAXERS

Do I feel guilty about taking time off from work? If so, why? I have suggested some possible causes that I think are operative in our society. How about you personally? Do you feel as though God will be displeased if you quit work an hour early to play a game of tennis? Are you afraid of what others will say if they feel you're not "carrying your end of the log"? Will you feel you haven't earned the time off? Will you be afraid that someone will think you're lazy? What about those reasons? Aren't they all a species of the need to prove ourselves, whether to God, others, or ourselves? How about just doing what you want to do for once? How about not having to prove that you've deserved or earned anything? How would that feel? Would that feeling make you more aware of who you are in Christ?

When do I really feel that my time is my own? What am I doing then? Sleeping? Or is there *any* time in the week when I feel, "This time is mine"? For instance, I tend to feel that my time is my own when I am doing something I don't have to do. As a result, when I am doing something with my children, playing with them, walking with them, or fooling around with them, I tend not to think of that as my own time, because I feel that as a good father I ought to be doing that. But in a real way this *is* my own time, and I am choosing how I will use it. So I need to work on my attitudes there. If I were to recognize how much discretionary time I really do have and that I am choosing freely how to spend it based on my priorities, I might feel less harried. Because, for me, whenever I begin to feel that what I am doing is an obligation, that tends to begin to drain the joy out. On the other hand, if I can feel I am doing something, whatever it is, because I choose to, the joy has a way of filtering back in.

At the same time, it is still necessary as we reeducate ourselves to find that time when we not only *are* free, but also *feel* free, a time without obligations. For it is in that time that we will be able to be re-created by the release of tensions and expectations and we can know again the joys of pure grace.

GOODS-INTENSIVE RECREATION

How dependent am I on goods for recreation? Do I really have to have the very best tennis racket in order to enjoy the game? Do I really have to have a super-expensive set of clubs to enjoy golf? As we follow the high-consumption patterns our society sets for us, we'll find that we spend more time buying and less time relaxing. We'll grow to have an increasingly casual attitude toward the creation. Because we are able to spend less and less time paying attention to any one object and because it's cheaper to throw things away and buy new ones than to repair them, our ability to value and appreciate atrophies. We may also become hooked on more and more expensive things in an effort to increase our pleasure.

What is the solution? I think the first step is right here—a realization and an assessment of what is happening to us. The second step is an act of the will. Let's choose by the grace of God—and it will take large amounts of His grace— to scale back our wants. Recognizing that the goal of the game is enjoyment, let's laugh at manipulative marketing techniques and buy the least expensive equipment that will give the proportionately largest amount of enjoyment. Since the development of the mind and the spirit is the least goods-intensive form of recreation, let's choose leisure-time activities that use the fewest goods possible. How about a long walk with a friend? Has anyone skipped stones on a pond recently? Or how about lying on your back imagining things in the cloud patterns in the sky? Sounds almost subversive, doesn't it? But it seems to me highly probable that the more dependent I am on goods, the less I am developing my mind and my spirit. Recently I heard some-one make the pungent comment that a person who goes to the mountains in a $125,000 camper is probably more inter-ested in the camper than he is in the mountains. Right?

This is perhaps the place to discuss the relationship between recreation and leisure. In many senses the two words are synonymous. They are both talking about the use of discretionary time, but recreation tends to focus more on activity, and leisure speaks more of attitude and approach. Recreation is but one element of leisure. To the degree that recreation becomes merely being entertained, it is moving further and further from true leisure. To the degree that our time is filled with people doing things to us, we have lost control of the direction of our lives. One of the most alarming elements of the current youth culture is their tremendous need for stimulation and their corresponding boredom with anything less than that super-stimulated state. Genuine leisure—re-creation—is very difficult for someone with such a mentality.

FREEDOM IN CHRIST

Now I would like to focus more specifically on our leisure time. First of all, how is my free time an expression of my freedom in Christ? What kinds of things do I have in mind here? Well, for instance, is there something you have always wanted to do that is really quite harmless but that you haven't done because "someone might not approve"? I remember several years ago two of our female friends went together to take belly-dancing lessons. Well, at first I was a bit scandalized. But then I got to thinking, why not? After all, they were not going into the business! Furthermore, the husband of one of our friends, discussing the results, wiggled his eyebrows up and down a couple of times and said he was quite impressed with his wife's progress. "For freedom Christ has set us free," Paul says (Gal. 5:1, RSV). Where are we ever to experience our true freedom in Christ from the bonds of worldly convention and respectability if not in our leisure? Please understand, I am not talking about sinful freedom which springs from rebellion against God. What I *am* talking about is that freedom from human expectations that is the birthright of the one who passionately loves Christ.

RELEASE FROM DRIVENNESS

Does your leisure time give you any release from drivenness? For instance, I find myself setting up goals for my "free" time. Today I want to accomplish this, or see this, or get this far. My wife and children accuse me that when we are traveling on vacation, I will not make an unscheduled rest stop until they are rolling on the floor of the car begging for mercy. After all, we might not make our schedule if we make too many unplanned stops! Now, I'm afraid that at my advanced age there is not too much likelihood of radical change in my patterns. But I can still back my goals far enough down so as to make it possible to enjoy the experience, the process, for itself. The other way, we are constantly frustrated because we didn't reach the goals or complete the plan, and as a result we're unable to enjoy the activity itself.

DISCOVERY OF THE WORLD

Is there any discovery of my world, or God's world, in my leisure time? Choose a particular interest in the world, one that has no bearing on your work, and cultivate it. This doesn't have to be something major or heavily time-consuming. For instance, Bishop Earl Hunt, presiding bishop of the Florida area of the United Methodist Church, tells of his long-time love affair with biographies. Of course, the insights gained from that kind of reading have been helpful to him in his lifetime of service in the church, but he says that's not why he reads this kind of book. Rather, he says, he does it because it opens up the world to him, giving him an appreciation for people and the world that he would not have otherwise.

But you don't have to feel compelled to do something as obviously "profitable" as reading biographies. As I said before, God's love for His world is not based on utility. Whatever it is, if it's a part of the world, it's worthy of your interest. Maybe you're interested in Greek archeology. Fine!

Develop that as a subject in which you have a modest expertise. The importance of such an enterprise lies not in what you can do with your knowledge, but in the very exercise of discovery. In that exercise you are becoming more truly human, more the learning, discovering, integrating being God imagined. How much better that you should be engaged in something like that than receiving another injection of anesthetic from the tube!

But perhaps you are saying, "I don't really have any interests like that. What about me?" First of all, I don't mean for any of these suggestions to become straitjackets. They are only ideas for how to give feet to some of the things we have talked about. Also, I don't think our interests in God's world need to be purely intellectual. For instance, an interest in gardening can be an open door to discovery of, and love of, God's world. As far as discovering an interest goes, you may need to sit down and just ask yourself and God, "What *does* interest me or what *could* interest me?" You may very well discover that you do have an interest, but have just never taken the time to develop it.

The list of possibilities is endless: botany, natural history, stamps, antiques, a particular person. Let it be something where your mind is engaged and where you can learn for the pure joy of learning. You are not after a grade; you are not out to impress anyone. You are walking hand in hand with God, coming to know Him better as you come to know His world.

Even if you don't have a special interest of your own, there are great opportunities in our culture for the general development of the mind and spirit. For instance, there are museums. Our culture has gotten us into the acquisitive, consumptive mode. Thus, we need to "do" a museum—see everything in the minimum amount of time. Let me suggest that you pick one room, period, or area and take the time to really absorb that. Just take one painting and spend some time with it. Do the same with a piece of music. It will be time well spent.

CREATIVITY

Is there any expression of creativity? What can you do that is creative? For most of us our work is not creative, but repetitious. We are doing the same things over and over again. For some of us, our work is very concrete and we can see the results of what we have done. But those results are so quickly undone. Karen tells me that she wouldn't mind cleaning the house if the rest of us just wouldn't mess it up again inside of 24 hours. Others of us may have work that is very challenging, but whose results are difficult to identify. We are people, all of us, who need some creative outlet. We need to participate with God in the making of something. We need to be able to do something and when we've done it say, "There it is. I planned it. I made it. It's not the greatest, but there it is." There are tremendous values for us in this sort of thing. So few of us today get a chance to see something through from start to finish, but in a creative project we can.

I don't mean that we can't use kits or plans. Anything that will get you involved in a hands-on project is good. Maybe you can do needlepoint. (And I'm talking to men as well as women here. When a 250-pound football player does nee-dlepoint, it's OK for us guys to do needlepoint!) If it's something you can do, by all means do it. Paint by numbers; maybe a "true" artist would look down his or her nose at that. I don't. You're developing a skill, making something. Better a lot more of us should be painting by numbers than that we should be killing each other over increasingly violent spectator sports.

Many of us feel self-conscious when people begin to talk about creativity. When we look at a Rembrandt or a Tolstoy or a Saarinen we tend to say, "Well, I'm just one of the drones, one of the worker bees." But just because some people are very talented should not deprive the rest of us of the joy of doing what we can. Earlier I mentioned the story of Mary anointing Jesus' feet with the costly perfume (Mark 14:3-9). In that story Jesus makes a striking statement. When the others grumbled that she didn't sell the perfume and give the money to the poor, Jesus said, "Leave her alone.... She did what she could" (Mark 14:6, 8, NIV). Remember that, according to John's Gospel, this is the same Mary whom her sister scolded for not serving at the table. For me, this is one of the great statements of the Bible on individual worth. Mary may not have been much good at serving or at helping the poor, but "she did what she could." It was something unique, something special.

In the same way, for each of us there is something *we* can do. It may be auto mechanics. Creative? Sure, and there's a deep sense of fulfillment that you feel when your car begins to run without knocking and clunking. "I've done that," you can say. "I've analyzed the problem. I've worked on it. I can see results." Woodworking. Gardening. Creative writing. Three or four young pastors of my acquaintance in north Texas and Oklahoma have a little round robin. They're all interested in poetry, so they write poems and send them to one another and send one another comments on the poems.

Each of us needs to ask, "What can I do?" Not what can somebody else do. One of the great evangelists of our day is a painter in oils. Most people who know him superficially would think that all he does is pray and witness, but that's not the case. This is a man who is free in Jesus. His life is not compartmented into work and play. All of his life is for the Lord, and that includes painting.

SILENCE

Is there any silence in our free time? One of the priceless commodities of our day is silence. In a real sense, we are only truly free when we have nothing to do, and no sounds are bombarding us. So if we are to experience God's freedom in our lives, we must find time to be alone with no demands on us. Most of us are involved with people much of the time, and we need time to be by ourselves. That's one of the values of a good devotional life. That means not just reading the Bible, not just consciously praying, but simply being silent in the presence of God.

For many of us in the evangelical tradition, one of the most iron-handed demands on us is that of regular devotions. As I travel and talk to people about their spiritual lives, one of the real guilts they share with me is the inconsistency of their devotional lives. God calls us to freedom. If your devotional life is merely a source of bondage, take a break from devotions, change your pattern, don't feel you have to do anything, just be silent before Him.

Of course, there are other ways to be silent. For some of us, silence is threatening. To be alone with the emptiness of ourselves is frightening. We have not developed our minds and our spirits, so the inner person has nothing to say to us in the silence. That's the situation with so many teenagers in our society today. Deafening, mind-numbing noise is far preferable to a silence filled with a dread of meaninglessness. If that is the case with you and me, there is a first step to deal with the problem. That is the act of contemplation. Go to a quiet place; if you can go for a walk, do. Pick up a natural object and look at it, really look at it. Study it in all its aspects. Let your mind range over it and follow out the various byways of thought that come. Let God talk to you in and through your thoughts. It will take a while for this mode of silence to bear fruit for you. Don't give up after the first try. There are real re-creative possibilities here for us.

FELLOWSHIP
Does our leisure time include fellowship? So much of our being with people is for some purpose other than just being together. It's a committee meeting, a business lunch, or a worship service. In my experience most women have less of a problem here than most men. Women generally tend to value people for themselves more than men do. All of us need to be with people for the sheer joy of it. There may need to be some structure to give our meeting direction and to keep us goal-oriented ones from being too uncomfortable, but the main point should be to be together.

I think of two such fellowship times that have meant a great deal in Karen's and my lives. One of them is a weekly couple's Bible study that has met in round-robin fashion in the homes of five or six couples now for 14 years. The central focus has been Bible study and prayer, but the dessert time afterward has been equally precious. When we. are meeting at our house, and Karen and I are in the kitchen getting the dessert on the plates, I listen to the murmur of the conversation, punctuated with waves of laughter, and know it is good to be a human being, a child of God, and a brother.

The second group of which we have been a part is entirely different. It's the Wilmore Book Club. Prestigious, huh? This is a group of 24 people who meet once a month to hear one of the members review a book. The only requirement is that the book be outside of the reviewer's professional field. What fun! There have been times when the freest I have felt in days has been at Book Club. The obligation to review only comes around once a year or so, and in between times you get the benefit of some books you probably never would have had a chance to read. And you also get to know your friends through their reviews in ways you couldn't otherwise.

An element I would not want to leave out here is family. Whatever else the family is about, it is about fellowship Recently I have especially appreciated Karen's fellowship. I am so thankful that in a large and sometimes cold world, there is someone who is for me without reservation and whom I can be for without reservation. Time spent with her is infinitely valuable, even if it's just going shopping.

The same is true for children. Our family is much like many others, I suppose. Before we had any children, I was an expert on child rearing. Now that we have three, I make it a point to keep my mouth shut on that topic. I really resonate with that bumper sticker that says, "Insanity is hereditary—you get it from your children!" Still and all, after Karen, the next best gifts from God in my life are our children.

I mentioned earlier that sometimes I don't feel like my time is my own when I am doing things with the children. Well, that's a good example of fact over feeling, because whatever I have felt, one of the joys of my life has been time spent with them. And as I have been able to view that time as fellowship, I have enjoyed it. Just to be with them—not to instruct them, not to teach them, not to straighten them out, but to be with them. Certainly that's what fellowship is: being with people.

In this matter of fellowship, find somebody, if possible, with whom you can talk about ideas: In my experience, much of our talk, professional or otherwise, is some form of gossip. We never get to concepts. Admittedly, that's pretty hard in a group of four or five people. There's just too much diversity. Oftentimes it will have to be you and one other. It may be a coworker, or someone you never see otherwise. It may be your wife or husband, but somebody you can talk ideas with and not just personalities or problems. That kind of mutual intellectual stimulation is a part of fellowship too.

PARTICIPATION

What about participation? Is my free time spent completely in passive occupations? Do I have two hours of genuinely free time each week? Do I spend all of that in front of the TV set? Or do I spend it all in reading grade-B literature? The big problem with these kinds of activities is that they are primarily passive. We watch other people doing things. Our minds are largely disengaged. We only do things vicariously. Now some of this kind of diversion is fine. Particularly those whose work demands a high degree of mental involvement find this kind of reading or television fare relaxing. Recently J.I. Packer, a noted evangelical theologian, reported that several members of the editorial board of *Christianity Today* were readers of westerns, thrillers, and mysteries. Personally, I found that a great relief; I'm not alone!

However, as I have said, if our entire free time is taken up with passive, diversionary activities, we're in trouble. We need to be active during some of that time, both as a fuller release of pent-up tensions and as an expression of our own significance. What form of participation can you be involved in? A regular golf foursome, tennis, a book club, some kind of craft organization, volunteering in social service, or any of a host of others—something you can do that is not merely escape.

How shall I sum all of this up? Above everything else, find time to be free. Make it. If you are totally driven, with every minute scheduled, you're not a very good image of Christian freedom. We all need to find that time when we don't *have* to do anything. However, having said that, I need to underline what all the authors on leisure say: there is no virtue in feeling compelled to play either. "Oh, all right, I suppose I've got to take this free time. I don't know what I'll do with it, but I suppose I'll find something." It is no part of my purpose to make people who really thoroughly enjoy their work feel guilty because they enjoy it and would rather do that than anything else, but I do want to open up the vista of leisure to people like that, so they can see the additional possibilities it offers. The fullest life is neither all work nor all leisure, but one that has a rhythm of both.

Bishop Hunt, whom I mentioned earlier, tells of the religious leader who told a company president of his acquaintance that he had not had a vacation in five years. The company president looked at him with a straight face and said, "Poor planning." Sometimes the real reason for our lack of leisure is not that we don't have time for it, but that our own vision of ourselves will not allow us to plan for it. If we can alter that vision and make those plans, what we find may exceed our wildest expectations. Work and leisure go together.

T H I R T E E N

LEISURE AND THE CHURCH

We come back now to the question, How shall the church address the problems and possibilities of leisure today? I hope you are convinced by now that leisure is something that is not only permissible from a biblical point of view, but is in fact desirable. I hope you also feel personally convicted and also empowered to make leisure a positive aspect of your own life.

If those things have happened in your thinking, then we are ready to move on to the church. I think the first step is to educate people. That education process must, first of all, involve the pastor. Our pastors must be men and women of leisure in the truest sense. Now there is a cruel myth about pastors, which is that pastors have a very soft life. After all, they only work three hours a week, at most!

THE LEISURED PASTOR

To be sure, a pastor has a very flexible schedule and has a fair degree of choice about how to parcel out the time. It is also true that if a person wishes to be lazy, he or she can make the pastorate a fairly easy life. But in my experience the lazy pastors are few and far between. Instead, I find many who are living with abnormally high anxiety levels because of the endless demands on their time. For instance, there is the never-ending requirement of sermon preparation. Unless we have actually had to do it, most of us have no idea how hard it is to come up with a fresh, relevant, spiritually stimulating sermon, or *two*, every Sunday, 48 or 50 weeks of the year. Add to that committee meetings, counseling, visitation, small-group ministries, and perhaps a Sunday School class and a prayer meeting. Then, when every hour of the day is accounted for, throw in some unexpected funerals, some family crises, a few weddings, and the town drunk who calls you at 2 A.M. to tell you at great length that he is drunk again and hates himself. The result is a person whose life is fragmented, who feels pressured, who feels that he or she never gets anything done completely. It's no wonder that selling life insurance looks increasingly tempting to many a pastor. It would be such a simple life!

Yet contrary to the advertisement for a preacher which appeared at the turn of the century, saying, "Needed, a preacher. Must have warm heart. Big feet. Preferably no children. No hobbies. Will work all the time," the pastor ought to be the most leisured person among us. This ought to be the person who can stand back from the pressures of life and, taking the long look, be able to tell the rest of us what matters and what doesn't matter.

Do you remember the story of Frederick? That's the sort of person our pastors need to be, men and women who can gather eternal values while the rest of us gather the nuts and seeds necessary to keep life going. If we drive our Fredericks to distraction, who will be left to help us lift our eyes to beauty and love and grace?

What this means is that each congregation must be sure that its pastor is protected, not merely for the pastor's sake, but for the congregation's own sake. We must insist that our pastors take time off and see that it is taken. Most pastors have a great need to be needed, and the thought that the church might be able to get along without them for a day is difficult. They will have to be reminded that they will fill needs better the rest of the time because of the time away from the pressures. Give them four weeks of vacation and try to see that they take it as a block. If we have a person in the pulpit who is at peace with himself or herself, who is free, the rest of us are much more likely to find peace and freedom too.

We also need to free our pastors as much as possible from the day-to-day operation of the church. Moses learned this at the beginning of the wilderness wanderings and the apostles practiced it in the early church. Other people can manage committees and finances; other people can ramrod building programs; nobody else can be the shepherd who can take the time to survey the terrain and show us, in the light of eternal values, how to live.

Recently I was in a lovely new church building. As I talked with the pastor, I was prepared to hear of the strain the building process had been on the pastor and the congregation. What a delight to hear him say that though there had been disagreements, all had been settled amicably. He also reported that he had had very little to do because the building committee had been composed of people who had gifts and experience in the building business and who had, in careful consultation with him and the rest of the pastoral staff, handled the whole matter. These people did not do this because they wanted to cut the pastor out, but because they knew the importance of giving him the leisure to do what he was called to do.

TEACHING GOD'S PEOPLE

When we have secured our pastor's leisure, then we need to begin to educate the congregation. The uppermost need is to help them see both the possibilities and the dangers that are before them and to show them that leisure is not something neutral to our Christian faith, but is directly in keeping with it.

Over and over again as society has moved and developed, the church has had to capture new movements, new developments, and new ideas. That must happen here too. Instead of bemoaning the fact that the automobile and the television and the 40-hour week have changed all our social patterns, let's help one another capture the new possibilities that are here for us.

In many cases, Christians are responding to these possibilities unconsciously, not realizing what's happening to them. Without haranguing them, without shaking our fingers under their noses and telling them they're all going to the devil, we can show them what some of the consequences may be if they choose or choose not to see leisure in a biblical context.

It is important to communicate that we are not merely trying to harness leisure because it has happened along and we are getting on the bandwagon even though we believe leisure is antagonistic to Christianity. No, we are saying that a correct understanding of leisure grows out of Christianity. As we have seen, the Christian concepts of grace, freedom, and creativity all call for leisure if they are to have their full impact. It is not necessary to choose between faith and a wise appropriation of leisure. We don't have to split the two, as though Christians work all the time, while it is only idle bums who play.

That split between work and play has created a tension in the minds of most people, predisposing them to choose the supposedly non-Christian option. Why? Because they think that's more "fun," and "fun" is a powerful motivation in our society. But we can say to people that they can experience the fullness of their Christianity within the context of leisure and can do it in such a way as to become the lords of their leisure rather than its slaves. Leisure, rightly understood, is fully Christian, more Christian, in fact, than some of the workaholism and some of the compulsive-obsessive attitudes that are sometimes called Christian.

AN AD HOC COMMISSION

As a further step, I recommend that the church appoint an ad hoc commission on leisure. Now before you close the book in disgust—I mean, who needs another commission?—let me emphasize two things. First, I really mean *ad hoc*. Put a deadline on the group and dissolve it when the deadline is reached. Second, give the group a very specific mandate. I would suggest three tasks. The first task would be to do some sort of survey. How much leisure time do people in this congregation actually feel they have? How are they presently using it? What abilities and gifts do people in the congregation have? How would they like to use them? This kind of information will help the commission get a handle on your situation. The next task would be to arrange for some kind of educational experience. The final one would be to suggest some specific steps your congregation can take to respond to the leisure crisis of our day.

For the education experience there are a number of possible approaches. Ideally the pastor should lead the event. This is true not only because the exposure to the topic will be good for him or her, but also because our churches are being overrun with "experts" who come in for a big splash and then are not around for the hard work of implementation.

I would avoid a really intensive kind of program. If you choose to offer a special seminar, don't pack it so full that people can't breathe. A series of Wednesday evening programs accompanied by a light supper would be one approach. Another might be a Sunday morning or evening sermon series. Yet another might be a Sunday School elective course. It would be the committee's responsibility, in consultation with the pastor, to determine how best to go about educating their particular congregation.

In this education process it is important to provide for some sort of closure. By that I mean some means of getting the knowledge gained internalized and applied to the lives of individuals. At the least I would think that the kinds of inventories included in this book should be completed by each participant, but more than that is probably needed. One possibility might be to close with a session in which the participants are invited to share appropriate actions and activities for individuals, families, and the church to undertake in light of what has been learned. Participants could then decide to undertake two or three of the ideas at each level. It is important at this point to be realistic—and leisurely—and not, in the enthusiasm of the moment, to commit to more than is possible or reasonable. As we parents know, the success of our children's efforts is normally determined by whether we can help them at the start to choose goals which, while challenging, are still reachable. Good endeavors are often doomed to failure by the very success of the selling job that got people interested in the endeavor in the first place!

MAINTAIN PERSPECTIVE!

When we begin to talk about ways the church can help people capture their leisure for Christ, we need to be very careful not to sell its birthright. With any program, it is very easy for the church to begin to make that *program* its first task. How easy it would be to say that our task is helping people fill out their leisure time! That is not the church's first task. The church is called to be a servant to the world, but there is a difference between Christians' being servants and the institution's being a service organization.

One of the great temptations of the church is institutionalization of service. As an institution we decide to set up a day-care center. The church as an institution is going to do this. Now who could be against such a good effort? But what will happen? I would be willing to guess that in very short order most of the staff will either not be members of the church or will be marginal members. Then the question arises, "Who's serving whom?" How about members of the church becoming involved with a community day-care program? Do you see the difference? There is a difference between the institution's paying nonmembers to perform a service and the members of the body of Christ becoming involved. I don't think the two are necessarily mutually exclusive. It's possible for church members to be involved in something the institution is doing, but I'm a little bit frightened of institutionalization of service that does not actually involve the congregation.

We need to be careful to remember that the church's task is to win the world for Jesus Christ and that everything else is auxiliary to that. This means that our strategy with regard to leisure will always be to find ways to use leisure opportunities to achieve our ultimate goal. For instance, if there is a state park nearby, hold a worship service there. This is a contemporary way of becoming "all things to all men in order to win some." It is also an example of the kind of thing I have in mind for the church's approach to leisure. We must not permit this attempt to help people use their leisure time to become a diversion from our main goal, but rather another means of reaching that goal.

ENJOYING GOD

So what are some possible actions the church can take? I don't intend to give a lot of directives here because every situation is different. However, I will make some suggestions as discussion starters. First of all, develop a style of worship that promotes the enjoyment of God. I don't mean by that mere pleasure in God—that's too cheap. But delight in Him, awe toward Him, ecstasy, whatever will lift the people's eyes to God. Without question a lot of tacky stuff has gone on in the name of celebration, and I'm not suggesting we do that. At best it tends to trivialize God and at worst it has actually diverted our attention from God to all those pretty balloons going up to the ceiling. But whenever we can release people from their drivenness and their tendency to use everything as a means to get at something else, we have helped them. The best way to do that is to make worship a time when people are motivated to enjoy God, to live in Him, to value Him, to see Him as supremely worthy.

PARTICIPATING

Then, emphasize participatory activities. I don't spend a great deal of time preaching against television, but I feel pretty strongly about it. You cannot create a nation of spectators and continue to have a nation with vitality and energy and vision. One of the things that I really enjoyed in the little town where we lived for the past fifteen years was the children's day parade each spring. It's fun to be a part of this town on that day and to be a part of a homemade celebration. It doesn't look a bit like Pasadena, California on January 1. It doesn't look slick. It doesn't look professional. It's even a little humiliating. But somehow that's us. And we're doing it—we're the parade. Those are my kids dragging that dog along behind them, or strutting along in their Cub Scout uniforms. I think a church ought to encourage that kind of community activity. Television, you see, kills it; we can't do it as well as those people, so why do it? Our cheerleaders don't look a bit like the Dallas Cowboy cheerleaders. So why have them? But the Scriptures tell us that even the sparrow matters to God; they tell us that every person's contributions are important to Him. Whenever we can foster that kind of participation in His name, we have drawn people one step closer to that vision of humanity that is God's.

In the same vein, church-sponsored sports teams are a possibility. Yes, I know the idea is fraught with problems: "How many times a month do I have to come to church in order to play?" and all that sort of thing. At the same time, it was a very good experience for a certain rather overweight and uncoordinated kid to play basketball in a Saturday afternoon church league. I didn't make many shots, and I made a lot of fouls, but there was something good about getting me out on that floor and away from watching the Harlem Globetrotters, or whomever, on TV that afternoon.

Have you had a Sunday School picnic recently? Given all the "demands" on people's time these days, maybe not many will come. So? Organize it so that those who do will find release and fellowship. Has anyone seen the pastor and the chairman of the board paired up in a three-legged race recently? Wouldn't that sight do everybody a lot of good?

On a slightly more serious note, what about sponsoring a

missions team? People have the time and many of them have the money, so let's capture that. Let's get them involved in missions in that way. If you have had missions teams go from your church, you know the transforming effect this can have on people as missions becomes real for them, in many cases for the first time.

A variation on this is a two-week summer trip for the youth, with one week being some sort of mission effort and the second week being a camping, hiking, or canoeing trip. I think it was Arthur Schlesinger who said, "The problem is that we are becoming a nation of vicarious satisfaction. We get our satisfaction from watching somebody else get satisfied." That's dangerous, especially for our young people. As you know if you've had opportunity to work with kids on backpacking or hiking trips, these can be precious times when you get close to kids, when they're stretched and strained a little bit to make it up that last hill and they can see you stretched and strained a little bit too. God can be very near in those moments, and some doors are opened that are never opened in any other way.

Could the church organize an employment pool for retirees? There are a lot of grandmas who would like to baby-sit. There are some men who could be really great at yardwork and at fixing automobiles and at other kinds of tasks. Would there be someone in the church who would be willing to act as a coordinator for that? They could let the congregation know that there are, say, five retirees in this church who have these abilities and would be interested in spending a certain amount of time at it. That's just one idea. It is going to be increasingly critical for us to find some significant ways of helping the growing numbers of retired people make their needed contributions to all of our lives. Somebody has said that the average retired man does all the fishing he's been dreaming of for 30 years in the first year of his retirement and after that sits around the house and feels useless. How can the church minister to these people in more significant ways than in organizing a bingo club?

MORE HARNESS THAN HORSE?

In keeping with what Linder has said about the harried leisure class, we need as a church to beware of taking too much of people's time, filling it up with meetings that are really not that necessary. Some years ago I heard an executive of my denomination say, "The problem with our denomination is that we have more harness than we do horse." If it was true then, it's doubly true now. Too much organization and not enough spiritual power. There aren't any easy answers for the problem of overscheduling, but one idea is to consolidate meetings and activities into one evening a week. When you talk about helping people with their leisure time, just filling up their time is not the answer. It's creative use of that time, positive use of it, that we're after.

LEISURE—CRISIS OR OPPORTUNITY?

What we have seen in this book is that the crisis is an opportunity for Christ's church. There is nothing about leisure itself that is in opposition to the Gospel. In fact, many of the central truths of the Scriptures are hard to comprehend apart from an understanding and experience of leisure. If we seek to find ways to appropriate the attitudes of leisure to help us fulfill our mandate from the Lord Jesus, we do not need to fear that we run the risk of being devoured by antibiblical concepts.

At the same time we must remember that every good thing can be perverted if God's people will allow it. Nature still abhors a vacuum. If people in North America and Europe have more discretionary time than they have ever had before, it is also true that there are hundreds of unworthy claimants for that time. Can we Christians come to the kind of healthy understanding of the relation of work and leisure that will make it possible for us to recognize the potential pitfalls and blessings and help others to do so as well? The history of the church convinces me that we will. We may not do it very efficiently; there may be a host of fits and starts. But God will triumph, and He will do it through His people. The only real question is whether you and I will be among that branch of His people who will be obedient enough for Him to appropriate leisure through us. Will we?